THE WISDOM OF WIZARDS

THE WISDOM OF WIZARDS

Insights from Leading Consultants

Richard Metzler
and
Jon Metzler

TROVE PUBLISHING COMPANY, LLC

Art direction/cover design: Paul Leibow www.egohead.com
Artwork: Ben Perini

Printed in the USA

ISBN: 978-0-9801736-0-4

Trove Publishing Company, LLC
633 Skokie Blvd. Northbrook, IL 60062

Email info@thewisdomofwizards.com

CONTENTS

Introduction

Put any veteran consultants together and the stories begin to flow....

EDITOR: Richard and Jon, what's this book all about?

RICHARD METZLER: This book is essentially consultants talking about consulting. We interviewed over 35 management consultants, mostly in their own offices. We intentionally left the interview open ended; that is, they could talk pretty much about what they wanted to talk about as long as the subject was consulting.

We asked, "Tell us your history, how you got into consulting, what does it take to succeed, who were your best and worst clients (without naming names) and why?" We also asked about travel, family challenges, recruiting and mentoring.

And as you would expect, we had no difficulties at all in getting consultants to talk at length about themselves and their businesses.

JON METZLER (laughing): In fact, it wasn't unusual for an interview to last up to three hours, and in several cases the discussion was continued in the local bar after business hours.

EDITOR: So this is not just another expose of the management consulting industry, correct?

RICHARD METZLER: That is correct. My sense is that we have far too many "insider" books on consulting that promise to tell all. And I think that they are for the most part pure bull. I was a consultant for over 28 years. If consultants didn't do a great job and if consultants didn't deliver as promised, they simply wouldn't be hired ever again. And that is certainly not the case. Consulting is a huge business and it is growing. Rather than create another "insider" book, what we have done is to let these consultants sit back and reminisce about their careers.

EDITOR: How did this book get started? Where did the idea come from?

JON METZLER: Oral histories have become very popular in recent years, and that approach led to the idea of a book about consultants.

RICHARD METZLER: And I had just left my life as a consultant and for the first time in many years, I had some time on my hands. I was able to call on contacts in the industry and to arrange meetings with interviewees with no problems at all. In fact, most were highly receptive to getting together and to the idea of the book.

JON METZLER: I had just returned from several years in Japan and I was thinking about what I would do next. The book presented an interesting and fun opportunity to work with my dad before I went off on the rest of my life.

EDITOR: So some of these discussions took place a few years ago, is that correct?

RICHARD METZLER: Yes, and what I find fascinating is that the stories told to us almost seemed timeless. When you read a consultant's story about a client situation that in some case took place 20 or 30 years ago, it could well have taken place yesterday. The wisdom of the story tellers is as good today as it was then. Some of the lessons learned are good for the ages.

EDITOR: Tell me how you went about it. What was the process?

JON METZLER: We set up the interviews which took place over a six-month time period. They ranged in length from an hour to several hours, including later trips to the bar.

INTRODUCTION

RICHARD METZLER: Consultants have three attributes that helped us with this project. First, our interviewees are very smart people. They were senior people, in their firms and you don't get to be senior in consulting unless you're very smart. Second, consultants have a very keen eye for the moment. That is what makes them great consultants and great salespeople. They see and seize the moment. And they remember those moments. Third, they are all great communicators and they talk. Veteran consultants are all great story tellers. Whenever consultants get together the stories just seem to pour out. And you'll see that the stories that are in the book are usually centered on a situation that was important or instrumental to the consultant. They remember these situations and they tell stories to make their points.

EDITOR: Where did the title come from?

RICHARD METZLER: According to dictionaries, a "wizard" is a wise man, one who is knowing, or very clever or skillful. A magician or a sorcerer really. Another definition that I liked is for an alchemist: one who can turn lead into gold. It seems to me that good consultants all have a lot in common with alchemists and wizards.

"Wisdom" is the accumulated facts, beliefs or traditions, or knowledge acquired through experience. In my mind, it's the big gorillas teaching the little gorillas about life and what is needed to survive and thrive. And this is what this book is all about, it's these senior consultants passing on their experiences, knowledge and wisdom to the next generation. If you multiply the numbers of consultants interviewed by their years in the business, we have roughly 1,000 years of experience, and hopefully some of that is passed on through their interviews.

EDITOR: What are you going to do with all the money that you make from this book?

RICHARD METZLER: All proceeds from sales of the book will go to support the Richard Metzler Scholarships that my wife Barbara and I set up, awarded annually by the Foundation for Excellence in Management Consulting in affiliation with the Association of Management Consulting

Firms. Each year, two scholarships are given to students studying for their MBA's at major universities throughout the world. That way we can help build future business leaders and yes—management consultants— of the world. If you're reading this book, and you'd like to apply, go to www.TheWisdomofWizards.com for more details.

EDITOR: Who were your story tellers?

JON METZLER: Stories from 33 different consultants made the final cut, although we interviewed about ten more. Their names and titles, either now or at the time we interviewed them, is presented below.

OUR STORY TELLERS

MICHAEL ALBRECHT	Retired, former General Manager, Consulting Services, IBM Consulting, North America
ALAN ANDOLSEN	Disceased, CEO, Naremco
WILLARD ARCHIE	Former CEO, Mitchell & titus, LP
ROBERT ARNOLD	Retired, former Principal, Towers Perrin
ANONYMOUS A	Retired, Senior Vice President, major strategy firm
ANONYMOUS B	Retired, Founder and CEO, major technology strategy firm
JAMES BLOMBERG	Retired, former Partner, The Metzler Group
CHESTER BURGER	Retired, former Chairman, Chester Burger & Co.
LANNY COHEN	Director, Cap Gemini Ernst & Young
WAYNE COOPER	Former CEO, Kennedy Information
MISHA CORNES	Former Senior Consultant, Booz, Allen & Hamilton
CYNTHIA DRISKILL	President, CDG & Associates
RAY EPICH	Retired, former Principal, Cresap McCormick & Paget
COBY FRAMPTON	President, Charles Brooks & Associates

TERRY GALLAGHER	President, Battalia Winston International
STEVE GOLDFIELD	Former Partner, The Metzler Group
ROBERT HAMMAN	Retired, former Managing Partner, A.T. Kearney
FORD HARDING	President, Harding Company
PHIL HENDERSON	Retired, Former Partner, Frank Lynn Associates
ALLISON JACKSON	Consulting Services, AT&T Corporation
JERRY JACKSON	President, FMI Corporation
ELIZABETH KOVACS	Retired, CEO, Association of Management Consulting Firms
MICHAEL LaPORTA	Retired, Partner and Global Leader, Deloitte Consulting
CARL LOBUE	Chairman, the Lobue Group
BILL MATASSONI	Former Partner, Boston Consulting Goup, McKinsey & Co.
JON METZLER	President, Blue Field Strategies
RICHARD METZLER	Retired, Former President, The Metzler Group
EDWARD PRINGLE	Retired, Former Executive Vice President, William M. Mercer, Inc.
PETER SCOTT	Retired, Former Partner, Scott Madden & Co.
CARL SLOANE	Retired, Former Chairman, Mercer Management Consulting
PETE SMITH	Retired, Former President, Watson Wyatt Worldwide
DAVID TIERNO	Retired, Former Partner, Cap Gemini Ernst & Young
GERT VAN DEE	Retired, Former Partner, Boer & Croon Strategy Management Group

-1-

Getting Started

"It just happened to come along."

FORD HARDING

Have you always known that you wanted to be a consultant? Are you unsure as to what field you want to enter? You might be surprised to learn that the majority of the senior consultants in our interview group (many of whom have 20 to 30 years in the business) say that they became consultants almost by accident. One business school grad on his way to a job interview stopped a stranger on the street to ask for directions and ended up getting a different job offer, in consulting. Another accepted a job offer from a consulting firm because the company that was his first choice pulled a switch on the position he was to have filled. Another didn't know what consulting was when he was first approached by an old friend with an invitation to visit his firm.

Many times the reasons for taking a job in consulting (or in any field) are practical and straightforward—like the need to pay bills. But often the reasons are more complex (and sometime more humorous) than mere happenstance or economics. One consultant attributes his career choice to the vagaries of love, or more precisely its logistics. Taking a job with a consulting firm was the only way to stay near his fiancée. But in another instance, taking an out-of-town consulting job was the only way for an interviewee to get away from an old romance.

Of course, others had more focused goals from the start. One contributor recognized early on his passion for problem solving. Another thought that he could do better than the consultants he himself had hired in the past, so he started his own firm.

Some saw consulting jobs as temporary stops on the way to bigger and better positions in corporations. But they were seduced by the business and ended up making careers out of consulting. A few others left consulting for a while but came back because they "missed the fun" or they weren't "psychologically suited" to corporate life.

As John Lennon once said, "Life is what happens to you when you are busy making other plans." This certainly was the case for these senior consultants. Here is how they found their way into consulting.

ACCIDENTS HAPPEN

Picked Up Off the Street

I got out of business school, and after a year and a half resigned from my job. I had taken a job in industry and found out that was not what I wanted to do with my life. So I resigned and relocated back to Boston. I had no idea what I wanted to do, and was quite disappointed, and perhaps even a little depressed, because I had gone to two years of business school to learn how to make good decisions and obviously my first big decision, which was a career decision, had turned out to be a bad one.

I spent several weeks trying to think through what I wanted to do, and visited with some old professors. I put together a résumé, and sent it to some headhunters. Then I got a call from a recruiter to come downtown because he wanted to meet me and while I knew the general neighborhood where they were located, I didn't know it that well. So I parked on a major street, but I wasn't quite sure how to get where I was headed. I stopped this fellow in front of an office building and asked him how to get to such and such a place. The guy gave me directions and then he began to interview me on the street! He knew the office I was going to was a headhunter firm. He wanted to know if I was looking for a job. Well, yes I was, actually, I said. He asked me what I did, what my specialty was. I said marketing, consumer goods marketing, which are how I thought of my professional identity in those days.

And I remember it clear as today. Hotdog, he said. I'm looking to hire somebody as a marketing consultant, to work right here in this building. A week ago he'd been appointed to head a new a marketing consulting practice, and was looking to hire an MBA who knew something about marketing. So he asked me if I could be back at 3 o'clock. That was on a Friday afternoon. On Sunday night, I was on an airplane to Texas for my first consulting assignment.

I'd like to tell you that I knew what I was getting into and why, but if I did I would be lying. I think there was actually a combination of factors at play. One was just that I needed a job. Number two was that I had no specific direction in mind, and therefore the kind of general comprehensiveness of consulting seemed to be as good as anything else at the time. Most of all, I was attracted by this individual who struck me as a very sharp guy who I could learn a lot from. So I think it was the combination of those three reasons that got me into consulting, more or less by mistake. Plus having to ask for directions.

CARL SLOANE

Sounded Like a Good Idea

I got my start in consulting through a professor at the University of Michigan shortly after World War II. I had been out of school for three or four years, and a friend of mine and I thought it would be interesting to start our own consulting business. So we arranged an interview with my old teacher, Professor Gordy, who told us he thought it sounded like a good idea. He also cautioned that it might be better if we had a year or two of experience first with an established firm. He offered to introduce us to what was then McKinsey in Chicago. We had interviews and were actually both offered jobs. I accepted and my friend came along about three or four years later. This was back in 1945. Later, the firm spun off and became A.T. Kearney. That was my start in consulting and I was there until 1975. I must have done about 600 assignments over the years.

The consulting industry was fairly new in those days. When I joined the firm, there were about 10 partners and 25 professional people on staff. Today, they must have around 2500 on staff. Obviously, it was a pretty closely-knit group in those days. Tom Kearney, our managing partner, had been associated with James O. McKinsey since 1929. I have the letter sent by McKinsey to Kearney confirming their initial agreement. McKinsey originally had his own public accounting firm in New York City, and Kearney was his first partner in their Chicago consulting group.

ROBERT HAMMAN

'It's Not IBM, Is It?'

How I got into consulting was very much an accident. It was in 1962 and I was working at a Ryerson Steel subsidiary and had just installed a computer system. I was also trying to finish my doctorate at Illinois Institute of Technology. I had completed all my course work and was getting ready to start my thesis. That was already in my twelfth year in school. I'd gotten my master's degree, gone into the Army, come back, gone to IIT for six years at night, taught classes there, took two classes a semester, and was 36 hours past my master's, all in operations research.

Because of my background, I wanted to get into a job where I could do operations research consulting. The only place I could think of was IBM, which had people they called "management science representatives." I went and talked to my IBM reps. They said, "You're the perfect guy. We want you to be a management science representative." So I signed up and told my boss at Ryerson that I was leaving. He said, "No, we want you to stay here. We've got another job for you. You can be head of information technology at Inland Steel Container, our parent company." Everybody was trying to talk me out of leaving. They had all sorts of ideas about how I could work on my thesis. But I said no.

I went over to IBM on a Monday morning and met with the branch manager. He said, "Before you begin as a management science rep, I've got a little project I'd like you to work on." I said, "What's that?" He said, "I want you to go over to the phone company and install another computer just like the one you put in at Inland Steel." I said, "Wait a minute. That's not what I signed up for. I signed up to be a management science rep, and I want to work on my thesis."

"I'll give you a $2,000 raise if you go to the phone company," he said. I said, "Thank you, I resign." He said, "How can you quit? You just started an hour ago!" "Hey, you just don't get it," I said. "By offering me a $2,000 raise on an $11,000 base, you obviously don't understand me. I'm not here to get more money. I'm here to do what I want to do. And I don't want to be jerked around five minutes after I start."

"Well, you can't resign," he said. "You just quit Inland." I said, "Adios."

As it turned out, I had interviewed with Cresap McCormick & Paget about three months earlier, and turned down an offer. I didn't really want the job at that time—I didn't want to travel. I called the partner and asked, "Is that job still open?" He said yes. I said, "I'll be right down." The next thing I knew, they offered me $12,000, plus a bonus at year's end if I stayed. So I signed on.

When I went home that night, my wife met me at the door. She said, "How's IBM? How do you like IBM?" I said, "I quit." She said, "You quit? What do you mean you quit? How could you quit? You've got five children, you know. You don't have a job, how could you quit?"

I said, "Oh, I've got a job. I signed on with a consulting firm, Cresap McCormick & Paget. My wife said, "Who?" "You know, CMP," I replied. She said, "It's not IBM, is it?"

And that was that. I started the next day and was off to Michigan for a little assignment. The snow was deep out there. The job also screwed me up because I couldn't get my thesis done. I was traveling all the time. So I never finished my thesis. I didn't get the doctorate. Unfortunate.

RAY EPICH

A Place to Go While Looking for a "Real" Job

I think most of the people in my generation who entered consulting just needed a job. I don't think it was an orderly, well-thought out process. Most people had industry experience somewhere and were considering a change of career or a different job. I suspect most probably looked at consulting as a place to go while looking for a real job.

Some of the transition we're seen in and out of consulting has to do with the profession being seen as a good place for career development. As a consultant, you get to experience a variety of things with many different companies. And if you happen to find a situation and company that clicks, well, things can happen.

A pattern has developed since the '80s. People enter the job market, go to a consulting firm, stay for three or four years there, and then head off to another job or to grad school. We saw some of this in the '70s, but not as much. Now, with most of the firms it is a huge program. In our firm, we hired up to 500 candidates a year; most stay only three to four years.

And with us there is always the promotion possibility. You can go from being a freshly minted BA to associate consultant, and if you're doing well and we want you back, we can offer a full ride to grad school, including tuition reimbursement. But the full ride is on a two-way street; you have to pay for the ride by giving us three years.

ANONYMOUS A

It Just Happened to Come Along

I got into consulting around 1976. I had been working for a public-private, not-for-profit partnership. The group was run by the top business executives in Chicago, the CEOs or presidents of the major corporations in the Chicago area. My particular function was in the job development area.

We were trying to attract business to Chicago and I was convinced that the group really didn't know much about how location decisions were made. It seemed to me actually that they were operating under some false assumptions. Additionally, I had done some work on a project with a location consultant and when they had an opening, I approached them about it and was hired. I began to see that perhaps this was an area where I could make a contribution.

It wasn't a terribly deliberate move on my part. I did not set out to be a consultant. It just happened to come along at a time when I was very anxious to change jobs. I had been interested in that gray area between the public and private sectors and location consulting certainly fit into that category.

I have to say, before I became a consultant, my impression was always very positive. I thought it seemed like fun and exciting work. Mentally stimulating. I've been a consultant ever since, except for two brief years as the director of marketing for an architectural firm. It's a big industry with all kinds of people and a lot of very good firms. Of course, there are also firms you wouldn't want to be associated with, as in most industries. But, overall, I believe consulting makes a major contribution to the economy and to society in general.

What exactly is it about consulting that keeps me going? I think it's a chance to make a real difference. You have the opportunity to work on things that are very important to the people you're working with. As I said, the variety in the work is stimulating. There is also that looseness of structure, which allows you to take things to another level, to stretch and do something different. You aren't constrained the way I think you often are in many large organizations.

FORD HARDING

That Gut Feeling

I graduated from business school in 1964 and went to work in information systems back in its dawn. I was working for General Electric (GE) in Phoenix and back then GE had a big computer division. The area I was in was involved in some very interesting programming and systems design work.

I did not like Phoenix, believe it or not. We lived there for about a year and were actually kind of poor. Phoenix is not a place for poor people, at least not if you want to enjoy what's there. Also, in the summer it's so damn hot and humid. Around this time I was also coming to the conclusion that being a data processor wasn't what I wanted to do.

Undoubtedly, I was influenced by the fact that my dad was a lawyer. Growing up, I was always around people in professional services of some kind. Maybe that's why, when I saw an ad for a consulting position at Cresap, McCormick and Paget, I decided to respond. They wrote back. If I was ever in Chicago, they'd like to talk with me. I also responded to an ad for a position at A.T. Kearney, which was brought to my attention by a search firm. That was another opportunity in Chicago. I actually ended up arranging four interviews in Chicago, all in one week.

One of the partners I met from A. T. Kearney was an old name in the business. He asked me which other firms I was talking to. Then he asked me how I was going to make my decision. Being the analytic type, I said, well, I've got this matrix with all these characteristics, and I'm going to do a systematic comparison of all the firms. He smiled. That's not going to work. He said I'd go through all of this analysis only to discover that there was little difference in what the firms do, who they hire, how much they pay, what kind of work they offer, and who the people were I'd be working with. I would in the end find no discernible difference between any of them.

Well, what would he recommend then? The partner said, okay, here's what I think is going to happen. I would go back to Phoenix with my matrix and my analytic method, and one night I'd wake up in the middle of the night. I'd have this feeling in the pit of my stomach, and I would just know, this is where I belong. Of course, he was absolutely right. Don't ask me why. But that's the way it turned out.

As to why I got into consulting, I think my systems background gave me something to sell. I liked the idea of using analytic abilities, which is built into the nature of consulting work. I was also very project oriented and everything in consulting is project oriented. You're also constantly doing different things, always learning, not doing the same thing over and over. There just seemed to be a number of aspects to consulting that appealed to me.

I don't profess to tell you that I thought all this through when I entered the field. It just sort of began by happenstance and gradually gelled in my thinking into the idea that this is what I should be doing. I did later spend 10 years in line management but otherwise consulting has been my career. The truth is I came back to it because, compared to line management, consulting is a lot more fun.

ROBERT ARNOLD

"I'm psyched!"

So I Gave It a Shot

I majored in accounting in college, which I really enjoyed. The college I attended had what they called a cooperative program that allowed juniors and seniors to alternate between working and studying every other semester. The program would find us a job in a management training program in our career area. For me that meant a position in accounting with a large grocery chain. I remember how much fun I had my first semester, learning about corporate accounting. Then it was back to school, followed by another semester working.

The second time around I was put on a special project with a consulting firm that shall go nameless. Let's just say the people at this firm couldn't if their lives had depended on it find certain parts of their anatomy with both hands. They didn't have a creative clue about anything. A couple of the corporate types and I actually pulled together the brunt of this project. We also watched as the consultants did presentations based on our work. As a result I got a very bad taste in my mouth for consultants.

Later, I went on to graduate school, served two years in the Army, then spent about a year as an accounting instructor and another year as an auditor. I was very happy. At the time, Ed Kangas, who was just about to retire as Deloitte's global chairman, was trying to attract people from the audit function into consulting. His thinking was to build some glue between the two units, and he was making offers to anyone on the audit staff with an MBA to consider transferring into the consulting group.

Well, I met with Ed and told him I wasn't sure. I thought the consultants had too much to sell. Besides, I kind of liked what I was doing. But I did tell him if he were really insistent, I would give it a try, as long as I had the option of a ticket back into auditing. That was okay with him, so I gave it a shot. On my first assignment I found myself working with Ed to develop a strategic plan for an insurance company. This was in 1973. So that's how I got started, and it's been so much fun, I've never looked back.

MIKE LAPORTA

Consulting, What's That?

I started out with a degree in mechanical engineering and a master's degree in business from the University of Wisconsin. Then I went to work for Inland Steel in a tremendous training program. A solid year in which five people visited every nook and cranny of a business. We would spend anywhere from a day to a week, going from the accounting department to the steel mills to the iron ore mines up in Minnesota and Wisconsin. For somebody coming right of college, I had great exposure to the entire picture of a large business.

I worked in the mills at Inland Steel as a foreman. The only problem was I couldn't stay awake on the midnight shift. They only ran two shifts and midnight to 8 a.m. was just unbearable. Nothing to do. So I decided to go back to school. Inland Steel had a paid tuition program and I got an MBA at night from the University of Chicago. I still have a tremendous appreciation for that. No question about it, a wonderful company.

I made the switch into industrial engineering and spent another three and a half years at Inland as an engineer. Around that time a couple of things happened that turned me toward consulting. A good friend of mine who was working for Heidrich and Struggles got me an appointment with Gardner Heidrich. Gardner gave me an hour of his time and when we were done with the interview, he said something like, young man, you ought to be a consultant. I think I said, what's that? I didn't have a clue what consulting was all about.

In those days, my in-laws happened to be living next door to a fellow by the name of Bill Hocking, an operating manager and director for a firm called Fry Consultants. Bill was not the senior guy but sort of at a vice president level. The firm was originally called Booz, Fry, and Allen but Fry had left and formed his own firm. Well, after meeting with Gardner, I started talking to Bill. I was very intrigued and I ended up joining Fry Consultants. We must have had about 25 or 30 professionals in the office, which in those days was actually a fairly good size. I don't know that the other firms at that time had offices that were much bigger. Every practice was represented: marketing, organization, recruiting, psychological evaluations. We had these small groups of about two to five people in all the functional areas of what we then called consulting.

As I remember it, the firm was still predominantly known for industrial engineering. Unlike now, however, when we have to take almost everybody we bring in and train them in what we do; it was absolutely a no-brain transition for me. I started an industrial engineering project on Monday. They were not doing anything really notably different from what I had already been doing at Inland Steel for three or four years. So it was "Manager, get out of my way, what do I need you for? Give me the five grand or whatever the project was sold for and let me run with it." In other words, it was a very easy transition.

PHIL HENDERSON

Tell Me Again, What Is It You Do?

I've been with FMI Corporation and its predecessor since 1968. I came to FMI kind of through default. At the time, the company I was working with had posted me to Richmond, Virginia. When I got out of the Army and went back to work, I worked in Richmond for a year before considering a proposal to move to New York for a different posting.

Well, my wife had no intention of moving to the city. That's why while I was in New York considering our options, she was in North Carolina looking for a house. Actually, I was not too keen on starting a family in New York, either. Needless to say, the wife won and it became my goal to get relocated to North Carolina and then find another job in the area. As things worked out, the company wouldn't pay my relocation expenses. I had heard about this other firm called Fails and Associates Limited from an old fraternity brother from North Carolina State, so I thought I would look into that. I remember asking him, "Tell me again what it is you do. What is this company you're working for? And, by the way, are they hiring anybody?" The opportunity was there with Fails so I took it.

When I joined the company in 1968, I was being paid $15,000 a year, as I recall, plus a bonus when times were good. It was a pretty good claim back then. In fact, when I got out of the Army in 1967 and returned to work, I believe I was making $850 dollars a month. So it was a step up to join a consulting firm.

JERRY JACKSON

An Economic Moment Determined the Path

I've had two stints in consulting, one intended, one not. I completed UC-Berkeley's MBA/MA-Asian Studies dual masters program in December 2001, which was not a good time to be finishing business school in the Bay Area. Armed with an insightful thesis comparing entrepreneurship models in Silicon Valley and Japan, I duly entered the workforce unemployed. I had an extra semester for the dual degree, and during that I had seen the 1999 and 2000 MBA classes get laid off, and the 2001 MBA class have their offers withdrawn. This was a path-determining economic moment for a lot of people. Some, who'd seen the bubble's brass ring be pulled away, really took a long time to find their footing. Others improvised and landed on their feet quickly. By the way, there's no institutional memory among MBA classes. Later classes don't remember this, and don't care. Why should they?

In January 2002 I visited Seoul, Tokyo and Shanghai. In Tokyo I met a bunch of old contacts and made some new ones. I also got my first post-MBA job offer, which I declined. In the end, my first post-MBA project was a writing job, which is what I had done prior to business school. Over the course of 2002, I took on a variety of US-Japan market research and market entry projects, and late that year joined Performance Analysis, a small firm focused on that very field. Some work was simple day-wage work. Some was commission-based. Some was on a fixed price basis. We weren't very picky. With that said, I turned down three job offers that year that required moving to Tokyo.

My favorite project of that period in retrospect was trying to sell a Palm peripheral into the Japanese market right after Handspring pulled out, and with Palm on its last legs. The electronics distributors got a good chuckle out of that. Nice product! Very novel. You're three years too late. That company went out of business, by the way.

I joined a wireless startup client full-time with the goal of getting more domestic experience and that paid off. I learned several trades and found a niche I really liked – the intersection of communications technology and policy. In 2007, after looking at joining another wireless startup as co-founder (and only non-engineer), I made the decision to found Blue Field Strategies, my firm. I saw several policy-driven themes in the wireless and broadcast markets and thought those presented a sustainable opportunity. I drove up to Sacramento to fill out the papers in January 2008. I'm happy to say so far, so good. It's been a blast. There's a virtuous cycle of getting smarter and better with each project. I get better, and my clients get better insight and results. Now it's a question of scale.

JON METZLER

MONEY COUNTS

Lo and Behold, I Had a Family to Support

Unlike some other people I never planned to be a consultant. At least that was not my original thought. I was on track to become a university professor in Renaissance humanism, studying for a doctorate at Vanderbilt University in Nashville when, lo and behold, I had a family to support and had to consider some alternatives. Consequently, I got into the administrative line with a public health department in Nashville, Tennessee. I did this for about five or six years, building an administrative services operation for the metropolitan government of Nashville and the surrounding county.

I had the good fortune to work with a medical director who understood a lot about administrative issues. He got his start in Dade County, Florida, which has a long history and experience with metropolitan government issues. He understood a lot and allowed me to work out a lot of my ideas about creating a strong, streamlined administrative operation. You could say it was a ground floor experiment in government efficiency.

Back then my wife was finishing her PhD and I decided I would follow her wherever she had to go. I had pretty much decided I would not continue toward my own PhD. I finished everything but the dissertation. But looking at the economics of it, I thought my wife would have a much better chance in the academic environment. Actually, that's how it worked out. I had seen how difficult it was for some friends of ours, couples who were both working in graduate or teaching areas, to both secure jobs in the same area and move through the promotional ranks together. My wife and I also had similar majors and academic interests, which only would have compounded our situation. So in 1976 when she was offered a job on the East Coast, I circulated my resume and also found a job with an organization called Naremco.

Naremco was a consulting firm that specialized in records and information management. It was administrative services type of consulting and a natural fit for me. All the experience I had on the government front lines was very much what these folks were into. So it proved to be a happy marriage and I've been there ever since I took over in 1986 when the founder retired and have gone on from there. Our client base is now very broad and includes about 80 percent of the Fortune 500. The work basically involves corporate headquarters issues and functions, rather than line or plant work.

ALAN ANDOLSEN

So I Took the Extra Thousand

I worked in my dad's business after I got out of school, followed by a stint in the Navy. I had an accounting degree and really wanted to be an auditor. In 1968, a friend of mine, a fraternity brother, called and suggested I try to interview with Arthur Andersen. I did and was very impressed with their approach. I liked their attention to people and professional development. I hadn't really seen anything like it before. They also said they would pay me $11,000 to be an auditor or $12,000 to be a consultant. I had a wife, one child and another in the oven, so I took the extra thousand. And that's how I became a consultant.

Taking the job meant moving to New York from Pennsylvania where I was then working. We didn't have any money and my wife was very pregnant and I had rented this apartment in New Jersey for $190 a month. It was a very small two bedroom with a leaky roof. We had two women of ill repute living below us who entertained people at all hours of the night. The first time my wife saw the place she cried. But it was the only place we could afford and we lived there for three years.

I'd been working in factories and had ripped all the pants for my suits.

So I had no suits, just sport jackets and slacks. Of course, you had to wear a suit at Andersen, so we scraped together all the money we had and I bought myself a suit. On the very first day of work, it rained. I mean it rained big time. And I had to wear that suit every day for two weeks, until I got paid and could buy another one. My wife ironed it every night for two weeks.

ANONYMOUS B

Show Me the Money!

I became a consultant when I was 29. At the time, I was doing well. I was with a large Fortune 50 company, getting all the promotions and the raises. I was doing such a great job I was getting raises of 6.36 percent over 15 months, which was 50 percent over the norm. Yet every one of my friends was making at least twice that. So I needed to do something different. I was in search of some dollars.

I went out and interviewed with A. T. Kearney and with Metzler & Associates, also with Kidder, Peabody. The latter had a great ad in the Chicago Tribune. It said, come make lots of money now. I thought, that's my kind of company. I interviewed with Dick Metzler at the old Metzler office. Dick said several things that stuck. One was that we're here to make money. They didn't put their profits into the walls or the flooring like some companies. I mean, Kearney did have this beautiful office and the Metzler office wasn't much but that was cool with me. I checked out where Dick lived and that impressed me so I joined. What can I say?

We had the best system. The more you billed, the more you made, and the more you then moved up the food chain. With every step up you got a huge increase in income. Naturally, everybody really believed in that system 100 percent and wouldn't do anything to mess with it. That's also why we would do some of the work we did: state commissions, jobs in the bayous, jobs where we'd end up getting chased by wild dogs. But that's another story....

JAMES BLOMBERG

More Money, Less Risk

How did I get the idea that I could be a consultant? Actually, it was someone else who put the idea in my head. An individual at a client site suggested I could do this on my own and put me in touch with the finder, the lead generator. But it was looking at the revenue issue that did it for me. I was paid little enough considering the potential consulting revenue; well, even if I worked very little, I knew I could equal what I had made before. But it was not only the financial motivation that I could make more money; it was also that there was very little risk associated with doing it.

I started as an independent consultant back in 1980. I knew only one product, a legacy mainframe system for payroll personnel and benefits. I didn't even know it very well, but I knew something and hung out a shingle. Actually, most of my early work came through a finder, someone who had contacts in the business. I started at $250 a day, and he took half of that. But I learned the craft, as it were.

In the early days, most of my experiences involved doing internal training for companies. What would happen often is that I would then be invited to stay and do longer training engagements. In 1986, I consulted for the Pillsbury Company on a project that was larger than any I'd ever done. I realized at that point I was going to need more than myself. So I incorporated in 1987 and hired four people. Three of the four are still active with our firm, and here we are today with almost 100 employees and revenues of not quite $20 million. In fact, we recently won an award as one of the 25 fastest growing companies in Dallas. All these years later we're now in the emerging business category! Of course, today I'm involved exclusively in running the company. The last active consulting activity I did was at the end of 1994.

Yet there were several early years when I worked very little. Times were tough. If I weren't booked six months in advance, I wouldn't believe I was ever going to work again. I would never believe the future bookings were going to happen. If there was a gap, I would panic, believing I would never fill it. I could never really believe I had any money other than what was in the bank. I didn't know it at the time, because I didn't have a network of consultants to draw on, but I found out later that we all tend to feel that way when we first start out.

Actually, one of the reasons I started the company was that I was lonely as an independent. I was working an awful lot and I had contact only with customers. There is a jargon in our industry and I was expert at the jargon. But I didn't have anybody to talk to as a peer. When I started my company in 1987, one of the things I thought I'd find was some relief from this loneliness. I'd have other people I could talk with about the systems and the work, other people who kind of walked on my side of the street. Well, as you probably know, I found out that it's still lonely at the top! It's just a different kind of loneliness.

CYNTHIA DRISKILL

I'm Going Out With a Dallas Cowboys Cheerleader

I wasn't sure at first I wanted to be in business. I had graduated from Harvard College in 1968 with a degree in English literature but hadn't really thought much about what I wanted to do. I had a couple of offers to teach in Denver. Of course, this was during the Vietnam War when there was a possibility of being drafted. I knew if I were drafted I was going to go. You don't get raised in Western Pennsylvania and become a conscientious objector. That's *Deer Hunter* country, after all. But teaching did offer a deferment so that's what I did. I taught for three years and did a lot of creative writing. Later, I got a high draft number in the lottery.

I had gotten into stocks and bonds around this time and found myself thinking, well, if I'm going to be in business, I really ought to go to business school. So I went back to Harvard for my MBA. Honestly, I thought business school was a joke. It was a lot of one-upmanship and very little good teaching. I had people teaching production because they had a background

DILBERT: © Scott Adams/Dist. By United Feature Syndicate, Inc.

in the Department of Transportation, even though I don't think they would have known a factory from a train.

Later, after I got my MBA, I joined a small not-for-profit consulting firm in Washington, D.C., founded by Lever Brothers. They were involved in marketing for social causes. It wasn't just public service advertising but involved some serious thinking about how to motivate people to change their behavior, in regard to their health and other issues. It was actually great training for what I've since done in consulting. How to inspire people to do things when money isn't involved is a very interesting marketing challenge. I worked there for a couple of years until I joined one of our clients, United Way of America, which had hired us to write their football spots.

I wrote and produced for two years. In 1980, McKinsey contacted me about becoming their director of communications. I remember saying to them, "Well, that's fine, but I knew you guys in business school and you didn't like me then and I didn't like you and I'm not interested. Besides, I'm going out with a Dallas Cowboy cheerleader tonight. We just did a television spot for their organization."

Well, I thought that was that. But they called back three weeks later. Apparently, they had called every major public relations firm in town and couldn't find anyone who was the right fit. They still wanted me on board. Again, I repeated that I wasn't interested. But now they offered to double my salary! Well, at that point I said I'd do it.

BILL MATASSONI

They Seem to Make a Lot of Money

My interest in consulting goes back to when I was attending Wharton School of Finance for my MBA. During the spring of my first year I ran into a friend of mine who had graduated from Lehigh with me. He had become an accountant with Price Waterhouse. We were having a drink together and he told me about a bunch of guys wandering around the halls. He said, I don't know what they actually do but they seem to make a lot of money.

That sounded good to me and I said, "Do you think they hire people for the summer?" He had no earthly idea so I wrote to Price Waterhouse, to Peat Marwick, and to Cooper's. Price Waterhouse never responded. Peat Marwick said contact them when I graduated. Cooper's invited me in for an interview. My graduate training was in industrial engineering and I had already done an acquisition of a small industrial engineering consulting firm. About two weeks after the interview they called to offer me a summer job.

So I started out with Cooper's and worked the summer, liked it very much, and returned that January after graduation. I found out later that the person who had hired me was this wily old partner who was the most conservative guy I've ever known. Apparently, he wasn't going to put his money on the line before he knew that my time had been sold. So before he would offer me summer employment, he took my résumé and went out and sold my time to a client. My first job that summer involved sampling work in a refractory plant. We were trying to improve their management and material handling equipment. I got a good suntan, lost about 10 pounds, and learned something about living on the road.

And, in spite of all that, I went into consulting.

ED PRINGLE

LOVE MAKES THE WORLD GO ROUND

The Places Love Leads Us – Version I

I don't know that when you go to college you say, I want to specialize in management consulting. If you ask me why I got into this business, I would have to say it was really because of love. Early in my career, I was the eastern area financial manager of American Hospital Supply Corporation, which was a great company to start out with. It was a Chicago-based organization, very market-, customer-service driven, with a 30-percent compounded growth rate. It was also where I met my wife, which in its own way led me to this career in consulting.

When I was hired, I'd survived this arduous open-interview process where we were required to talk about ourselves for an hour, with TV cameras going. Ostensibly, the interviewer was himself being evaluated for an HR class, which is why the cameras were there. But, of course, what would happen is the VP of HR would ask the class to evaluate the candidate. They'd look at your logic flow, image, voice inflection, whether your tie was crooked. I mean, they would just rip you to shreds.

Somehow I survived through all this and took a job, eventually being promoted to a field location in New Jersey. This is where I met my wife. She was heading up customer service. I was such a workaholic I think she felt sorry for me and wanted to help me. So she introduced me to all her friends and I dated all of them until she was the last person standing. Then we started to become good friends amidst a frenzy of 75-hour workweeks, when there wasn't much time to play anyway.

One thing lead to another and when I was promoted again, this time back to Chicago, that's when I realized the feelings we had for each other. So I had to make the decision between career and love. My wife is a native New Jerseyan and said she would come with me to Chicago, but I could tell she was hesitant. I thought perhaps I should try to explore other opportunities within the organization. I looked into sales but just had a terrible feeling about hospitals. It was such a sterile environment. I thought I'd better steer clear of that, even though they were great jobs. I mean the products sold themselves. The reps made over $100,000 a year (this was back in the 1970s). But I had to be honest with myself and say, not for me.

As luck would have it, I had met the vice chairman of Peat Marwick consulting at a Beta Gamma Sigma function and ended up sending him a résumé. About three months later, I got a call from him. Or I should say, I almost didn't get the call from him. My wife was home painting the house and answered the phone on the 13th ring (pre-answering machine days) and I got the news that they wanted to interview me.

The rest is history.

TERRY GALLAGHER

Where Love Leads Us - Version II

My story is not one of having mapped out a clear career path in consulting. It's much more mundane. I graduated from Lehigh University with a degree in electrical engineering. I'd done fairly well in school so there were many opportunities. Unfortunately, the one thing I absolutely did not want to do was anything involving engineering. I had good grades in the area but knew I was would be the world's worst engineer from a mechanical or actual application side.

Instead, I looked for business jobs where I would be able to apply my engineering degree. I was looking at positions with IBM and GE and some of the blue chip companies. For personal reasons, however (my grandmother was very ill for a long time), I decided I needed to find a job in the Philadelphia area, at least for a time. That's how I ended up working for PECO Energy. At the time it was called Philadelphia Electric Company.

I wasn't interested in energy per se, but it just happened to be the right geography at the right time. I also thought it would give me the opportunity to go to school at night and work toward my MBA, which I did at Temple University.

So I worked there for about four and a half years, until 1990, and progressed through a number of entry-level and lower level management jobs.

Frankly, I think I was quite naive about consulting back then. I didn't understand what consultants did and had absolutely no aspiration or inclination for the business. In late 1989, however, McKinsey was hired by PECO Energy and I found myself working alongside their consultants. I recall they had somewhat of a rarified air about them, and everyone knew they had firm access to our CEO. I was becoming aware of the McKinsey model, but quite frankly I was somewhat disdainful of it. That was where I was at then.

Another personal situation also intervened to influence my career direction. I had been dating a great woman, a local Philadelphia gal who everyone loved, including my parents. Well, at one point she moved back home with her folks for a couple months, for reasons I didn't fully understand. I eventually learned that there had been this whole sort of confluence of events involving a medication she had been taking. It had really deep-sixed her and she was hospitalized. It was the saddest thing in the world.

I visited her for many months during her hospitalization. Later, when she went home, she surprised me by telling me she wanted to get married. Honestly, I had never been thinking about that. I also knew it would never work. Unfortunately, she couldn't accept this and began stalking me, at home and at work, calling me all the time. I just couldn't get rid of her and it became a terrible embarrassment. She was a nice person but I don't think she really understood what she was doing.

I had the opportunity to talk to a recruiter during this period. Well, the next thing I knew I was offered a management consultant position with the Metzler Group in Chicago. To tell you the truth, I didn't care about the profession, the romance of travel or the money. None of that mattered. I didn't even have my MBA yet. What I did have was a way to get out of Philadelphia! So off I went to Chicago. Six months into my appointment in Chicago, the firm received a large consulting contract back in New Jersey, close to Philadelphia. I had an obligation with the firm to finish my MBA program, so it worked out for me to go back. The project lasted about eight months, long enough for me also to get involved with someone else back there. Consequently, when the project ended, I faced a situation where I had to either go back to Chicago and possibly risk ending the relationship or decide to get engaged and married. I chose the latter course.

As you know the lifestyle of a management consultant is one in which you're often traveling five days a week. The good thing about that is that it means you can live almost anywhere. Because my fiancée had a job in Philadelphia, we decided to move back there. And that's my personal story of how I got involved in this business. It was anything but a preordained path.

STEVE GOLDFIELD

FIRMLY FOCUSED

Interested In What Makes a Business Tick

I got into consulting because I was interested in the operations side of business. I joined Arthur Andersen in 1968 right out of college, with my degree in accounting. The normal path for someone like me would have been to join a CPA firm and go into the audit side of the business. But I knew even then that I did not want to be a practicing auditor. I was more interested in what makes a business tick, and how to go about improving operations, as opposed to focusing on the numbers or what had taken place in the past.

At the time Andersen was moving heavily into what is now called financial services, but which then was simply known as the brokerage business. The firm had made the decision to train a group of people within the consulting practice who could support the brokerage audits from a systems perspective. They told me if I came aboard, I could go straight into this group. Of course, I said yes. I didn't hesitate. The irony is that I did very little of the data processing audit support work, which had been the reason this group was set up. Ninety-five percent of my time was spent in the brokerage industry doing straight consulting work.

What made me as an undergrad want to go into consulting? It's been so many years now, I honestly can't remember more of the specifics, other than, as I said, just being interested in the operation issues. I do know it's been a decision I've never regretted. I spent fifteen years at Andersen and was a partner in another consulting practice for four more years before I left the business. In terms of a career decision, it's been a great experience.

Of course, I've also had the experience of being so frustrated at times with a client that I've said to myself there's got to be a better life. I would imagine most of us have felt that way at some time. You find yourself wanting to retire about three times a week. That hidden desire comes up to just open up a bookstore and sit out front in a rocking chair with some mint juleps. But you get over that. This has been a good profession for me. It's been a constant learning experience and I really have no regrets. My older kids are in the consulting profession now and that was their choice. Of course, I suspect I had some influence there.

WILLARD ARCHIE

I Thought I Could Do Better

Prior to starting our firm, I had been working for Citibank. I knew that I wanted to do something different. My own experience as a buyer of consulting services was that they were always promising me A, B, and C. I would get half of what they promised and it would cost me twice what they told me it was going to cost. Well, I said to myself, you know, I'm sitting on this side of the desk and I'm the one always paying. What if there were a consultancy out there that would actually tell you what you need, what you're really going to pay, and deliver what they really said they would? Now, wouldn't that be something revolutionary?

That's basically the premise that we started our business with. Let's have a firm that focuses not only on looking good and telling people what they need to do, but on actually implementing things. Let's give people more than pretty reports. So we started the firm with this idea. We were very tactically oriented. We'd go to a client and do a free walk-through, spend three or four days and come back with a very focused proposal. That's how we worked. We'd say something like, "You know, we just looked at this area and we can restructure this for you and run it for $5 million a year less. Our fee to do this job will be so much, and it'll take us a year to do the engagement."

Interestingly, when we got started I had picked out this nice high tech name, and a friend of mine who was a bank senior vice president asked me why I had picked this name. I said, well, I guess because it sounds impressive. He said no, if you want people to believe you're really in this business, put your name on the door. They'll take you a lot more seriously. So we became Hamman Associates. And for 17 years we were Hamman Associates until we formed a holding company. Now we are Hamman Holdings LLC.

Something else interesting. When I started, I said to myself, I'll do this for about five years and then get into something else. That was 18 years ago.

CARL LOBUE

STAYED A LONG TIME

My God, How Did This Happen?

Initially, my thinking had been that I would never go into consulting as a career. I thought I wanted to do something more entrepreneurial. But I had applied to business school when I was in college at Stanford, and at the time business schools sometimes required people to work for a few years before admission. They would leave a position open for you, which meant I was admitted two years down the road.

I looked around for the job I thought would offer the best training and ended up taking a position with Bain & Company. Being a consultant seemed like a great opportunity to learn, to be exposed to a lot of different industries, and to be paid while learning about different emerging opportunities. Still, I thought I'd just be in the business for a couple of years.

While I was working at Bain, a few of the people there left to start another consulting firm, called the Monitor Company. They were working with Michael Porter, the Harvard Business School professor. I went on to business school first but later ended up joining Monitor, which became known as a young, hot consulting firm with one office and plans to open up many more.

Even then I thought I'd work just long enough to pay off my student loans. In the meantime, I'd figure out what I really wanted to do. At least that was the plan. Well, I ended up spending almost ten years there, until 1995. I woke up one day and realized I was about to celebrate my tenth anniversary at Monitor. I thought, 'My God, how did that happen?' I must have enjoyed it a lot more than I ever expected.

Eventually, I left with a colleague and another partner, who happens to be my brother, to start our own investment group. I had been doing a lot of work in the information and publishing industries, so we went to some private investors and raised enough capital to buy and build specialty information businesses. In 1995, we started our company, called International Information Investors. About nine months later we acquired Kennedy. [Editor's note—Kennedy Information is the publisher of Consulting Magazine. It has since been acquired by the Bureau of National Affairs, Inc.]

WAYNE COOPER

Psychologically Unsuited for a Regular Job

I was at the University of North Carolina working on an MBA with the full intention of going to work in the forest products industry. Between my first and second years, however, I ended up working on a consulting project with a professor that involved assessing the market potential of a product then called the Power Whip or the Weed Whacker or something like that.

It was an interesting project and the professor, whom I got to know pretty well, suggested that I consider going into consulting. So I added a few consulting firms to my interview list for the fall. One thing led to another, and I ended up going to work for Theodore Barry & Associates. Before I went back to graduate school, I had worked for three years. So I did have some work experience before I got into consulting. But I had very little real knowledge of what consulting was until I got into business school. Even then, I think I learned more by going on interviews than from anything else. Actually, consulting was still a fairly new industry back then, with roots in industrial engineering and the think tanks of World War II. I suppose what appealed to me at the end of the day was just the chance to rub elbows with a lot of smart people in the industry and be exposed to a lot of different companies. Still, my thoughts at first were to just go into consulting and work at it for two or three years, then parlay that into another job.

Of course, what happened was I stayed at Theodore Barry & Associates long enough to become a partner, which was almost five years. I was made a partner in September 1981 and then resigned in November to work for a client. So I did kind of end up doing what I thought I was going to do, which was to leave and go into industry. I went into industry only to discover that I had become, as a result of consulting, psychologically unsuited to be in a bureaucracy.

I realized within the first couple of months that I'd made a terrible mistake. But I stayed there for almost two years until I could eventually work my way back out. At the time my employer, who had previously been a client, was gracious enough to say, "If you want to start your own practice, we'll be happy to be your first client. You can continue working with us." I quickly turned that into, "Absolutely, thank you very much. I will now start my own firm." And that's what I did, in 1983.

PETER SCOTT

<figure>[35]</figure>

-2-

What It Takes to Succeed in Consulting

"A high level of intelligence."

MICHAEL LAPORTA

Consulting is a demanding business, one that requires a unique blend of intelligence and people skills. It also requires a variety of personal attributes that may seem contradictory at times: analytical abilities, confidence, competitive spirit, creative thinking, objectivity, attention to detail, big-picture thinking, and a personality that thrives on change, or at least is highly adaptable. Did we mention that it's a demanding business?

What does it take to succeed in consulting? The most successful consultants are likely to have integrated many of these traits and skills into the mix of what they have to offer their clients, enough so to keep them coming back over the years for more. It's not a sales trick. The best consultants convey to their clients a strong sense of their own authenticity: they are their own men and women. We suspect also this is what most clients want, even if they don't necessarily always know it – outside expertise that is confident, grounded, and willing to assert itself in its capacity to understand complex organizations, people, and problems.

What does it take to meet these challenges? Here's how integrating these skills and attributes well can translate into a successful career as a management consultant.

INTELLECTUAL FIREPOWER

The Consultant Is a Problem Solver

Number one, the consultant is a problem solver. You have to have that sense of curiosity. You've got to be intellectually honest. Over the years I've really had very few problems in this area, as far as the people we hire. I believe the selection process has been a good reason for that. The curiosity issue is what keeps them up to date intellectually.

I think people have got to be smart in different ways. It's not pure IQ. The term we use here is insight. You've got to have insight. Ironically, because of this, a person's background is not a criterion for hiring. Some of our best people have actually come from unusual backgrounds. One person no longer with us came from the CIA. My guess is that the CIA had a much better method of recruiting and identifying skill sets than we did and he was on their information desk. Stuff would come in to him and he'd sort down the 10 percent that was important, see patterns in it and then pass it upstairs. So working with this ambiguous information environment was a no-brainer for him. He was just very quick.

PHIL HENDERSON

Jacks or Better Intelligence

In poker, you have to have jacks or better to get in the game. In consulting, you have to have jacks or better intelligence to get in the game. And, by the way, there's a lot of room above jacks or better. So jacks or better isn't that high a hurdle rate but that's for openers. Second is just good common sense. I've known some brilliant people whose common sense coefficient just wasn't there. I think we all went to school with someone like that, the kid who was the brightest in the class, who could do just amazing things but who was just out of it. That kind of brilliance is not successful. It's jacks or better intelligence, street-smart common sense, personality, good listening skills, and the ability to understand what the clients perceive they need and want.

ANONYMOUS A

Just Because You Know Certain Things
Doesn't Necessarily Mean You Can Consult

I worked with a woman on a project in the Ukraine. She was a team resources expert, an older, kind of grandmotherly type, and she had spent her whole life thinking about how to make employees happy. She appeared to be an expert but, in fact, she was rather useless as a consultant. Just because you know certain things doesn't necessarily mean you can consult. You might find a person who seems perfect for a project, based on the body of knowledge they've crammed into their brain over 20 or 25 years of work experience. But then they lack the flexibility to parlay that experience into something that's workable for the client. It's hard for many people to bridge that gap. Yet that's what makes for a good consultant. This human resources person was useless in consulting, but she did teach me all about human resources policy.

There was another guy we hired, a Ph.D. economist who was supposed to help us in Ecuador on a project involving restructuring their power sector. Well, he knew the right answers about what best practices were. He knew how to deal with transmission tariffs, operation tariffs, replacement generators; all these technical issues that come into play in power generation, particularly when you're talking about nationwide power. Ecuador is not that big but there were all kinds of technical, structural, and economic issues, in terms of the way that you can price electricity. This guy knew all this, with a Ph.D. in the field.

And the clients hated him. They hated him because he insisted on pushing the particular vision that he had. He wasn't flexible to developing structure, which intellectually he was perfectly capable of doing, which would have suited what they wanted. This was someone who should have been exactly the right person for the work but was not.

MISHA CORNES

Consultants Are Really Just Great Appropriators

I believe consultants are really just great appropriators. What we do is appropriate a framework from another industry or client situation, from work we've done elsewhere. We take that framework and say, "How can I use this somewhere else?"

And that's how it works. Good consultants are always looking for things they can appropriate to their work.

JERRY JACKSON

The Very Best Are Intellectual Entrepreneurs

I think generally today consultants are at the far end of the curve intellectually, analytically, and conceptually. They enjoy solving intellectual problems and puzzles. In fact, they'd rather try to solve an intellectual puzzle than run something.

I don't think many consultants go into it with the notion of a career, but rather see it as an opportunity to learn more and apply what they've learned conceptually and theoretically in business school to real world problems. And in doing the work they gain the extra benefit of exposure, of added possibilities for networking. So you're talking about people who initially don't have a tightly targeted career direction, so they're very open to the expansiveness of the consulting profession. At the margin, the very best are intellectual entrepreneurs.

CARL SLOANE

A High Level of Talent

I think managing consultants is easy. Some people would say it's hard, but I think it's easy. If you really think about how complex the service is we render, it's remarkable how little we have to direct what to do. What we actually do is set a goal for the consultants on a team and it becomes up to them to figure out how to solve the specific problems. It is not as if we have to explain to every consultant on a team exactly what he or she must do, or what questions he or she has to ask. The reason that we can do this is that we hire people with very high levels of talent.

What would I consider a high level of talent? It's the usual things like creativity, diagnostic skills, being a quick study, a self-starter, mental agility, communication skills, presence, integrity, and teamwork. In our firm, no matter what skills you've acquired, you will not survive if you're not highly talented. Our firm takes the view that you can't improve someone's talent. Of course, you can always develop further skills in the talented. You can even develop skills in the untalented. But you can never increase the inherent talent level. That doesn't happen.

MIKE LAPORTA

PEOPLE SKILLS

The Ability to Tune In

A good consultant, first of all, must know something about more than the specific project or subject at hand. Without knowledge and some experience you can't do the job. But I think being able to listen to your clients is probably the most important thing. It's a talent. The ability to tune in, be creative in your thinking, do some lateral thinking. You have to be convinced that your contribution adds something, that the client will be better after you have been there. That's something that's in the best of us.

GEERT VAN DEE

Sensitivity Is an Aspect of Being a True Leader

To be a true consultant, you're not just going in as a know-it-all. Obviously, you do need to know a lot. Your knowledge is a very important part of what you offer to the marketplace. But there are an awful lot of other things that are important, too.

It's about relationships. It's about listening skills. It's about bringing an understanding of what it means to change an environment. It means techni-

"I don't know how it started, either. All I know is that it's part of our corporate culture."

cal competency. It means people development and how you bring them along. It means sensitivity to people. You are really the catalyst for change in many situations and change does have an effect on people in one way, shape, or form, whether their jobs change or are redesigned or even eliminated.

I remember when we were all going through re-engineering and major downsizing in the late '80s and early '90s. I'm only speaking for myself, but I know that there was a lot of sensitivity required. You had to recognize that at the end of the day, your work was having a material consequence on people's lives. The situations we were in spoke to a different aspect of who you were, or I should say, who you had to be. You had to be more than the cold-hearted consultant who comes in, announcing, "We're running these mathematical formulas and as a result of the benchmarking, as a result of best practices, we have concluded that you should be able to do this function with X-percent fewer people." We had to recognize full well that the results of those conclusions would lead to people being relieved from their employment.

This sensitivity is an aspect of being a true leader in the consulting business. We have to be people who come in with more than just technical knowledge or documented best practices.

LANNY COHEN

Listening Skills Are Number One

Something the consulting industry has been criticized for is having these 27-year-olds with MBA's, who've never really been on the other side. I mean, how can these guys consult? Well, I've been one of them. I believe that even when you're just starting out you can still be a very good consultant. But you either need to have supervision from somebody who has had that experience or you have to develop that understanding by really talking to and listening to the clients. I don't think necessarily they have to have lived the life of the CEO. Very few people experience the life of a CEO of a Fortune 500 client. But you need to have the ability to listen well enough and read the signals enough to understand what kinds of issues you're dealing with. And so I think listening skills are number one. A lot of people say you have to be a good speaker and presenter to be a good consultant. But actually I think the more senior you get, the more important being a good listener becomes.

WAYNE COOPER

The Secret to Success Comes from Within

My advice is to be your own person. In this business, you're going to get all kinds of advice, and the advice is often going to conflict. People are also going to ask you to do way too many things. To succeed you just have to be confident in your capabilities. That doesn't mean overestimating your capabilities, it just means being comfortable with yourself.

Consulting is about your capacity to engage the client, to be interesting and to bring energy into a situation in a comfortable way. Not to be buzzing around, irritating people. It's about the right level of self-confidence. You can't be afraid to ask questions or admit you don't know something. In the end, consulting is just about whether the people in the room like you.

You also have to be willing to invest in yourself. You have to want to learn something about the arena you're in. You have to develop yourself. If you're in this for a career, you should be thinking about how you're going to grow each year. Give some thought to your professional and personal goals. I believe the secret to success really does come from within. I don't want to call it a Zen thing because I don't know what Zen means. It's just some kind of inner focus that you have to have.

BILL MATASSONI

PERSONAL ATTRIBUTES

That Competitive Drive to Achieve and Excel

The type of person most attracted to consulting is the competitive person. There's that competitive drive to achieve and to excel. If you don't have that, you don't last long in consulting, because you're always going to be faced with the challenge to deliver.

Another characteristic is to be thorough, to pay attention to the details. There's the data and the importance of making sure you have the data; making sure that you've analyzed it and looked for trends before you make any recommendations. Of course, we're talking about not only data issues but in some cases the politics, too. Whatever recommendations you make have to be based on the full facts of the situation.

Basically, you've got to be thorough. You don't want to shoot from the hip. That's the bottom line.

MICHAEL ALBRECHT

If You Find Yourself Going Native, You're in Trouble

I think a good consultant has to maintain his or her objectivity. If you find yourself going native, you're in trouble. Objectivity is critical. I work exclusively in the insurance industry and my clients have anywhere from 6,000 to 100,000 employees. They don't really need one more person who knows about the insurance industry. They've got thousands of people that know about the insurance industry. What they do need are people who can be objective without fearing that their jobs are in jeopardy.

MIKE LAPORTA

Keep the Clients at the Top of Your Organization Chart

The skills I see as inherent to success in our business are essentially project management skills. You've got to be able to handle five, ten, fifteen assignments simultaneously. Most likely they're going to be fifteen divergent clients, too, with divergent needs and personalities. Relationship management is a part of this and it's critical. So you've really got to be part psychoanalyst, too. If you don't keep the clients at the top of your organization chart, you have no organization. To be able to meet new, prospective clients, gain their trust and confidence, and have them give you that first chance to deliver on a critical assignment, that's relationship management.

Unfortunately, what we deliver is not like a hard building or a system. It's a service. I think one of the unique aspects of our growth, why we've grown so significantly is that we have the ability to keep the client at the top of the organization. Plus the person that sells the engagement owns the engagement. He or she is the project manager accountable to the client's success. We reduce that to writing in our contracts. We guarantee to work with our clients until they deem the engagement a success. So that puts us over the barrel of accountability. As a result, about 83 percent of our work is repeat work from past, satisfied clients.

When I left Peat Marwick, I wanted to go with an organization that had the same kind of process controls in place, one that really wanted the clients as opposed to the revenues. I've found you can ascertain very quickly where a firm is at when you're being interviewed and they ask, first, what are your billings? And, second, who are your clients? You know then where the emphasis is going to be. That's what you see with a lot of firms. As opposed to talking about the importance of managing clients, about cultivating clients for ten, fifteen, or twenty years, trying to limit the number of assignments to a level you can physically handle, and keeping the reputation up.

Consulting is all about managing expectations, and communication skills are critical. I think some people in our business do this pretty well. But there are also those that are just deplorable. It's the old don't-shoot-the-messenger issue that comes up. The client may have this element of expectation about his or her needs, and then there's the real world that you find on your consulting engagement. So it's up to us to continually educate and update the client so that the gap between what he or she thinks they need and what we may be actually finding doesn't widen. If it does start to fester, I submit it's more important to be in front of the clients when that gap widens than when it lessens.

It is human nature to say, oh, this is getting out of hand, it's going to be an ugly meeting and they're going to yell. But if you manage the process in weekly increments, you can never be that far apart because you're giving them your work in vitamin pill bits. But if you go for three months and the gap is widening and they're still expecting you to deliver, that's when all bets are off and it can get real ugly. Some consultants don't handle this well.

TERRY GALLAGHER

You Want to Be the Alpha Dog

So what does it take to be a good consultant? I think a healthy ego and the ability to be forceful and express your opinions. No one pays a consultant to be wishy-washy about stuff.

Oddly enough, I've noticed there's some sort of perverse pride consultants take in killing themselves. It's not so much a perverse camaraderie, I would say, as it is more of a culture of one-upsmanship. You want to be the alpha dog. That's actually why partnerships work so strangely, because you have a bunch of alpha dogs trying to make things work.

MISHA CORNES

Good Consultants Have a High Fear of Failure

I believe most consultants who do good work have a high fear of failure. They are insecure and this drives them to work very hard on behalf of their clients. The mindset that will ruin a client relationship is when consultants forget to be fearful of failing, when they boilerplate the thinking, believing they can package what they do and get away with it.

This work, when it's done right, is never repetitive and never boring, if you look for the unique characteristics in each and every situation. Every individual client you deal with is different. As human beings, they are always different. Every business situation is different. If you look for those distinctive factors and try to understand them, the work will always be fascinating. But the moment you start using standard recipes, that's when it becomes boring.

I suspect consultants who are in this business for the long haul are easily bored. They require that constant sense of stimulation, that feeling of engagement. Maybe we're all a little affected by attention deficit disorder. If a client relationship doesn't offer that stimulation– that is when the relationship is going to be a truncated one. Because we no longer have our brains engaged.

JERRY JACKSON

Confidence, Trust, and Listening

I'd say there are three things that are important in my experience. One is a clear sense of confidence. I'm sure there are consultants who have maybe gotten by with just bullshit. But I think you need confidence because you need to have a combination of depth and width. Clients want you to be a mile wide and a mile deep, and you know you can't be both. And to me that's where the confidence comes in.

The second thing is trust–the ability to trust, to generate trust, and to keep trust. It boils down to the reputation you build through your honesty with clients, and through your willingness to tell them when you can help and when you can't help. One potential client called once about a job in Italy that they needed handled in a very specific way. I had been trying to get to them for years, and they finally called with a job for us. But they wanted someone fluent in Italian who knew executive compensation factors. I called them back about two days later and said, "I've done a lot of digging, and I found your man. He's fluent in Italian, he knows compensation, and he's done work for a lot of competitors of yours in the industry. He knows the industry. The bad news is he works for our competitor."

"Why are you saying they're better?" she asked.

I had to say to her, "Because there's nobody in our firm that can meet your requirements. We do have somebody who does compensation, but he doesn't speak Italian."

So they hired Towers for that assignment, but they started hiring us for a lot of other jobs. Because, as they told us, "If you're going to send work to one of your arch-competitors because it would help us, then you do believe that when you can take something on, you must be able to do it." It took a while, but our relationship with that client took off. So that's trust.

The third thing is listening. There are a number of consultants who talk much more than they listen, and I think they miss the mark.

PETE SMITH

Short Span of Attention

In some ways, being a good consultant requires having a short attention span. By that I mean you need to have the kind of focus that thrives on constant change, constant turnover of people and challenges. Obviously, you don't always have a lot of time to do what you have to do, and you need to be ready to move onto the next thing. When I've been involved in long-term assignments, I have often found it emotionally hard to walk away because I've gotten to be such a part of the situation. And that's probably not healthy in the long run.

So if you're a person who thrives on change, then you're a good candidate for consulting. But I turn it around and call it a job where it pays to have a short attention span.

ROBERT ARNOLD

DILBERT: © Scott Adams/Dist. By United Feature Syndicate, Inc.

It's About Life-long Learning

As far as I'm concerned, you cannot be a management consultant if you're not open to life-long learning. I mean there are others who will say, I'm just consulting because I have this natural ability to do X, Y, and Z. That's fine. For me, what it's about is life-long learning. What I've learned didn't come out of Rutgers or MIT.

Consultants are also people who like to teach. That's a very important thing. Consulting has people who like to impart knowledge to other people and feel good about it. I have my own database of 30,000 people worldwide that I started when I was a dean at Princeton. It includes engineers and scientists from all over the world. So I don't know everything and I don't have to know everything. I just need to know who knows it.

Being a successful consultant requires personal integrity. You've got to like yourself.

My husband and my son call me an elitist, but I do think you need a high educational level. I'm not saying there aren't successful consultants who aren't highly educated. There are. But in the technology age we're in, more and more education will be required.

I also see a need for strong people skills. By that I mean knowing how to interface well with all kinds of people. Having that global perspective. A successful consultant should also be someone who by nature is less biased. I don't mean less biased just in terms of race, but less biased in terms of being able to look beyond certain things about people. Like their education level or the part of town they live in, the clothes they wear or how much they weigh. The consultant who can do that is going to be a better consultant.

ALISON JACKSON

You'll Forget the Paycheck After You're There Two Weeks

If you don't really enjoy the work, there's no way you're going to want to put up with the sacrifices you have to make as a consultant: having to run your social life around your job. It's impossible to be a consultant and organize your job around your social life. There are real sacrifices. You have to enjoy the challenge of achieving things and getting things done. That's what we look for.

I often hear people say, "Oh, I want to be a consultant because it pays good money." That's a crock, because you'll forget the paycheck after you're there two weeks. What starts to really come home is what you're doing, the work content. That's the nature of the beast.

CARL LOBUE

You Measure Yourself by the Success of People Who Work for You

I think you measure yourself in consulting in two ways. Over the short term, you measure yourself by the success of individual assignments, and collectively by the success of clients you worked with. Over the long haul, however, I think you measure yourself by the success of the people who work for you. As I look back, I think more in terms of the people who worked for me and what they are doing now. The high points are when people who worked for me go on to have major business success, whether it's been in consulting or in a corporation. I'd like to think that I've made some contribution to their development and growth. Conversely, the low points obviously are the people who you thought had great potential but who flamed out and did not grow.

I'm really pleased that some of the people who used to work for me are now CEOs of companies. That feels good. I mean, you'd like to believe that you had some contribution, whether it was in coaching or just exposing them to opportunities for self-development. But then you think back on some people you thought had high potential and for one reason or another they never really achieved that potential. You wonder if you could have done a better job with them.

ED PRINGLE

Basically, a Consultant Needs to Know How to Stand Tall

Sometimes the clients engage you to provide a prescription, other times to assist them in developing an answer. The latter is much more process-driven although you hardly ever want to label it as that. The former is much more brain surgery-driven, so to speak. This is the answer; this is what you must do. This is our prescription. Interestingly, the clients will pay almost as much for the "this is what you must do" answer as they will for the "process answer," even though the former takes a lot less effort on our part.

Of course, it also helps to be right, and in order to be right it helps to have a few years of experience. It's hard for younger or newer consultants to hand out prescriptions and be believable in that role. To some extent, you can coach credibility. You can talk about the importance of projecting confidence, how to do that. If I flinch when you challenge me on something, or get angry easily when you push back, well, these are things that can erode my credibility. To some extent you can coach people on things like this.

Of course, people also are who they are. Basically, a consultant needs to know how to stand tall. You have to be willing to be challenged, and almost enjoy the ideological combat. You also have to just be able to hold the client's attention.

JERRY JACKSON

They Remain a Bunch of Mavericks

The consulting life really gets into your blood. It takes a special kind of person to be a consultant. They're entrepreneurial personalities, people who are generally very sharp. They're their own people and are not impressed with Harvard MBAs or bluebloods or what have you. It's more an issue of what kind of person are you, and what can you do? They definitely have an independent streak and I think that they are just fun people. You have a lot of laughs. Everybody has a lot of stories. I would think perhaps more so than in more staid professions like the legal, medical, or accounting professions. Consultants run loose. Even in big organizations, they run loose. They remain a bunch of mavericks.

That's one of the key things about the consulting field—people are paid a lot of money for their hard work and services, as opposed to being paid for pure brainpower or pure intellect. As opposed to being paid as an investment banker by your luck in the market. Consultants make money off their hard work, their tenacity, and their commitment to a client 24 hours a day, 7 days a week. Clients unfortunately take precedence over so many other things such as family and personal life. That's different from many other professions.

In the end, you obviously need problem solving skills. But perhaps personality traits are more important than anything else. Intellect is very important, but not necessarily intelligence as measured by an MBA or CPA or advanced degree in engineering or anything like that. Obviously you need common sense and strong people skills, a sensitivity to your environment and the politics around you. That's absolutely critical.

It also helps to have tenacity and physical stamina and a very understanding family.

ALEX ZABROSKY

AND IF ALL ELSE FAILS, THERE'S ALWAYS LUCK

Be In the Right Place at the Right Time

There was a guy named Sonny who had started a new limousine service in Washington. He started out with one car and some clients that he had been serving from a previous job and he built the limo service up. By the time of the story his little business was growing—he was up to eight or ten cars. One day as he took me out to Dulles Airport, Sonny said, "I'm really excited because I'm picking up Andy Grove, the founder of Intel. I'm going to try to pump him for information on how I can do better."

On his front seat he had a copy of Grove's book, he had magazines with Grove's picture on the cover, he knew how much Grove was worth and that Grove was the fourth richest man in the world. Sonny kept citing all these statistics to me – kind of like he was practicing for when he'd finally meet Grove.

Finally, he dropped me off at the airport and I wished him good luck. Four or five days later when I returned Sonny picked me up. Of course, I asked him, "Sonny, how was the ride with Mr. Grove?"

"Oh, he was a fine gentleman, just a wonderful guy," Sonny replied. "But it was somewhat disappointing."

"In what way?"

"Well, after the small talk I finally got to what I really wanted to ask Mr. Grove. I said, 'Mr. Grove, what I'd really like for you to tell me is how I can be more successful in my business. With all of your vast experience and success you must have some advice that would be helpful to somebody like me, just starting out with this small business.' Mr. Grove sat in the back seat for a minute just thinking. And then looked at me and said, 'Be in the right place at the right time.'"

I thought that was an interesting comment. People who are successful often have this sense of their timing. If they're right about it and they probably are, then success is just so much luck. Because three feet over to the left and the other guy gets the break and you don't. It's fairly capricious out there. You just have to be at the right place at the right time.

PETE SMITH

-3-

Rating the Client

"I loved all of my clients. It's just that I loved some more than others."

RICHARD METZLER

onsulting is ultimately about the clients. Our senior consultants clearly understand that without the client there wouldn't be a business—that without them, consultants wouldn't exist. And so they love them all, deeply. But it doesn't mean that they love them all equally. What makes a client stand out as a favorite? Per our veteran consultants, most highly valued and remembered are those clients who are smart, educated and knowledgeable; who have vision and direction; who want to do well; and who set high standards for themselves and their organizations. Consultants also highly regard those clients who are realistic; who are open to change; who love their jobs and work hard; and who possess a sense of integrity. And lest we forget, consultants really love those clients who have large budgets and who pay their bills on time. In contrast, our contributors were equally clear about those clients that they did not like or respect – those who are dictatorial, who are not accessible, or who lack courage. Many of our interviewees also talked about clients who use consultants as alibis, or who are fraudulent or prejudiced. Many were clear that working in the public sector was at the bottom of their preferences. We can see that there are many red flags that say, "Stay away." Sometimes, however, turning away work can be hard.

DEFINING THE GOOD CLIENT

A Client Who Is Focused

A good client relationship begins with clients who are focused in terms of their objectives. When I think back over the years, the projects I had difficulty with were usually the ones that weren't properly defined. In many cases, the client wasn't quite sure what he or she was looking for. So a good client has some clarity about what his or her needs are. Your deliverables are more easily defined. The client is open to what you have to say.

The worst clients are the ones that don't want any criticism. Or they only want criticism of others. They make terrible clients because invariably they will fight you on your recommendations. It's not likely they're going to implement anything. But then, when nothing changes, the scapegoat, of course, is going to be the outside consultant.

Let's face it. If you're saying change from A to B, this implies that A had issues, that something was wrong. Obviously, the nature of our work is that our analysis and recommendations may be critical of the company we're working with. So it's always best if you have clients who are confident in themselves. You know they can handle criticism or more readily accept your recommendations. That's what I look for in terms of a good client.

It also helps if they pay their bills promptly.

WILLARD ARCHIE

RATING THE CLIENT

A High Degree of Trust

I think a good client is a client where there's a high degree of trust. The client has issues to address and you know you can make an impact. There's enough trust to take risks and make things happen. Those to me are the best clients. One of our largest clients today is a major investment bank and that's the kind of relationship we have with them. We have a number of relationships like that. In some cases, our clients become business partners. So, it's a different way of operation, and one that requires that level of trust.

The big red flag is when there's that lack of trust. When you really can't make an impact, no matter how hard you may work. That's why I won't do government work anymore. Government tends not to be trusting of the private sector. The civil service people and even the political appointees often have the attitude that they have virtually nothing at stake. They don't have the same incentives or context. You can't operate in environments like that. I know this is generalizing, but government work in general is just hard to deal with.

ANONYMOUS A

Not Jaded or Cynical

The best individual client I ever worked for was a vice president at Allegheny Power. He had visibility within the corporation so by association; I did too. He was a smart guy who wanted to do well. Until then he hadn't dealt with consultants in his entire career so he wasn't jaded or cynical like some other clients. And as a result, we did a good job for him.

We had a great team there. They felt we moved the company forward. I think we moved the company forward. We even got recognition in their annual report. It was just a straight-up assignment where it was a hell of a lot of fun and we did some good.

Sometimes with other clients there were so many consultants involved that it was chaos. Consultants were running the company but not in name, and so different projects were competing and vying for attention and direction and emphasis. It could be kind of a joke sometimes. But Allegheny wasn't like that. That was the only time in my career when we had a client who had never worked with consultants before. We were positioned to do a strategic project that senior management took seriously and they gave us the latitude to make it happen. And it was great.

JAMES BLOMBERG

A Client Who Is Committed

A good client has a clear understanding of what kind of help he or she needs. He or she also has a realistic sense of what the likely outcomes will be. So good clients are usually educated clients. There is also trust. They trust their consultant. There's also probably some flexibility.

What often happens in consulting projects is that initially you go in to solve a certain kind of problem. And then you realize that the identified problem is not really the main problem, or is just symptomatic of a bigger, underlying problem. A good client understands this and learns to be flexible and is willing to make adjustments in mid-process.

What is probably most important is a client who is committed to providing the support to execute the recommendations. So many consulting projects are just left on the shelf. They're not executed and end up having no value to the client organization. Good clients gets involved enough during the course of the process so they retain ownership of the project, they're committed to making things happen, and they don't wait until the end to either accept or reject the consultant's recommendations. If there is a problem along the way, they jump in and get involved early on. After all, they want the final outcome to be useful to them.

WAYNE COOPER

Moderately Confused copyright Newspaper Enterprise Association Inc.

Absolutely Loved Their Work

I can share one story that was particularly memorable. I had been working with AT&T for years. On one occasion in the '70s, they brought me in and sent me to the Bell Laboratories. Now, at that time, Bell Labs was perhaps the greatest scientific research institution in the world. I had never had any contact with science before. I had no education in the field of science and actually had no interest in it at the time. All of a sudden, I'm meeting these great scientists. I mean, two of them were Nobel Prize winners.

These men were probably in their 50's or 60's at the time. You could still see the excitement, the intellectual excitement of these men, even after a whole career. They couldn't wait to come to work in the morning. They absolutely loved their work.

I don't mean just those two Nobel Prize winners, either. All of them were like this. These scientists were so excited by what they were doing. It opened to me, for the first time in my entire life, an interest in science that has grown ever since. So the variety of consulting work has really stretched me to acquire new interests, and to learn new things. It's a continual learning process.

CHESTER BURGER

A Willingness to Partner

You can have all the talent in the world, but if the people in the client organization do not want to work with the consultant, it's not going to work. If the client doesn't feel a sense of engagement with your company, then you're going to have to either fix the relationship, or you may as well not be having the engagement. There has to be that sense of purpose and a willingness to partner. To work together well also entails honesty and openness and a responsibility on the part of the client to be constantly monitoring the quality of the relationship.

The other side is that the consultant shouldn't want to take over. You know the old saying, "Give a man a fish, and he eats for a day. Teach a man to fish, and you feed him for a lifetime." Being a good consultant means being an enabler, in the positive sense of the term. It means creating, maintaining, and fostering initiative and competency on the client's part.

Of course, in the immediate sense, you may want to just teach them what fishing is about, letting them know that for now you'll do the actual fishing. But your client certainly has to learn what fishing is about. They need to know what they're buying. Good clients understand this.

ELIZABETH KOVACS

Who Will Speak On Your Behalf

How I define a good client would depend on the mission and the number of repeat assignments we have. Referring us to their friends would also be nice. I guess perhaps the ultimate client is the one who will willingly speak on your behalf.

We used to sponsor seminars on particular topics and invite interested companies in the area to attend. These seminars might cover some new, unique technique one of our staff people had developed, which we were trying to publicize. Sometimes we would ask someone from one of our client companies to speak, which we found a great way of telling others about our methods of doing business. Let the clients testify on our behalf, so to speak. It usually proved to be a good source of business.

ROBERT HAMMAN

Who Is Realistic

Good clients are those who are realistic about what they can or cannot do. They're willing to work with you within whatever limitations they have. They have reasonable expectations and live up to their end of providing whatever resource or data or opportunity we need to work with their people. They're also willing to discuss and come to agreement about the changes that have to happen. And then live up to those agreements. Basically, what makes a good client is someone who is reasonable and who is knowledgeable.

Of course, many of our clients we've worked with for years. When they call you, they often already know what the problem is. Most of them already know generally what the solution is. They just need help in zeroing in on it and putting it together. On the other hand, you have difficulty with those who think you can do a $50,000 job with $300. Or make statements like, "I could do that in a week." The temptation is to say, "Well, you've been here five years, why haven't you done it?"

COBY FRAMPTON

Clients You Like, Clients You Respect

There are clients you like and there are clients you respect, and those are two different feelings. The clients you like are the ones who give you a lot of latitude. They're not telling you what to do all the time. They say, "Here's the problem, you guys go solve it." How exactly we do that, how we allocate our resources or time, is pretty much left to us. The client takes a hands-off approach, limited only by some broad parameters. They also don't question your invoices.

The clients you respect are the ones who really manage the process and you as a consultant. They clearly demonstrate that you work for them and they seek to get the best and the brightest out of you. But they also give you that same latitude. By contrast, some clients can get lazy with consultants and just expect us to do all the work; they kind of give the problem to us. Then, when you make the presentation the client will, so to speak, just say grace around the table, in terms of either yea or nay. They don't usually outsource the decision-making process per se. But they will outsource much of the work that leads up to a decision.

The reality of things is that if clients are not involved in the process of formulating and working through the problem and solution, then it's hard for them to make an informed decision. They're just being steered by a presentation.

STEVE GOLDFIELD

Very Good Business People

A good client is one characterized by interaction with very good business people. I've especially liked working with middle market companies, small companies. Maybe it was just my style, but I never worked well with big bureaucracies and procedural things. I liked to deal directly with top management. In our business, you can get stuck in the middle manager level where if they say they want a certain thing done and you discover the problem is really something else, they think you're just trying to sell them more. But with the smaller clients there was no disconnect between what really needed to be done and what they told you needed to be done. When you can deal directly with CEO's who are close to their business, in a hands-on way, they know what has to be done and they can respond more effectively.

One of our best clients was an ice cream company on the West Coast. Two consultants had bought out this little one-store ice cream place that had great flavors and turned it into a national brand. They were delightful to work with. One of their rules was that there would be no personnel department, no HR, none of that kind of bureaucratic overhead. The poor CFO, who was my primary contact there, had to get the HR stuff done without calling it HR. But those kinds of clients were the best I ever had. They were the types of clients who were usually very good friends and good to work with.

PETE SMITH

Their Guy Stood Up

The best clients know what they want and are willing to listen to your expertise. They're also willing to push back when they think you're going too far. As I've said, they have a clear understanding that they're looking after the best interests of the firm and the stockholders, as opposed to some self-serving agenda. They also understand they've bought you for your opinion.

I've had a lot of good clients over the years. I remember a project we did for a major aircraft parts company. We were locating an aircraft parts plant and they hired us to look at, among other things, the labor market implications of the decision. There was a town in Maine under consideration and in the course of our fieldwork, the head of the town planning department mentioned that this particular site was next to a trout stream with very strict environmental implications. You basically couldn't put anything into that stream.

I did mention this to the client, being concerned that they might not be aware of it. But somehow the ball got dropped and they ended up locating there. Later, when they realized they couldn't put anything into the stream but would have to cart stuff away in trucks, which had cost implications, they never blamed us for it. Of course, we had mentioned the environmental restrictions, but in a very casual way. I think it could have been easy for them to put the blame on us. I mean, one reason you get hired as a consultant is to bear the brunt if something goes wrong.

But their guy stood up and said, no, we were told. That took a certain amount of courage on his part. You have to respect that. They could have taken the easy way out and made it hard on the consultant. You know, we're getting a fair amount of money for this work. It would be easy for them to justify laying it on us.

So that kind of honesty and integrity in a client can only be appreciated. It helps if they're smart, too.

FORD HARDING

Give Me a Strong Leader

It is easy to identify a good client. Above all, I think the best clients have integrity. They know what they want and there's strong leadership at the top. That's the key to success. They tell you this is what I expect; this is what I'm looking for. You give them a proposal and you ask them, are you willing to go through with this? You understand what this is going to do to your organization? The pain involved? That we're perhaps going to organize some of your people out of a job and all those things. The best clients will say yes. And show the leadership to make sure that it gets done.

With a good client, there are no hidden agendas. We've had a couple of engagements where we were integrating different cultures after a merger. Everybody had his or her own agenda. Those are the engagements that can be difficult. People are not always acting with integrity. Instead everybody's trying to push his team, as opposed to choosing the right solution for the entire organization. I always say that creates smoke in the room. You can't see clear what it is you want to do. How can you when you don't know what the real agenda is?

I will say this, give me a strong leader and I'll take the project everyday. Most people are looking for signals from the boss. If you're doing a project, for example, and the guy running the business says, okay, I'll put this guy in charge of it, the first thing I ask is, what's his position in the organization? Is he someone who failed on the lines so now you're giving him this project to run? If that's what you're doing, guess what? I don't want the project because it's not going to work. They're going to say the boss isn't serious about this or he wouldn't have put that dip in charge. Isn't that the truth?

CARL LOBUE

Do They Need a Consultant?

Some of my best clients are those people about whom I initially think, why for heavens sake do they need a consultant? But they are the people who know exactly what they want from a consultant. They are absolutely clear in their assignment, in the way they conduct or ask you to deliver your work. It becomes a pleasure to work with them.

One of the members of the board of a certain company in the Netherlands was one of my absolute top clients. I've done two assignments for him. One was about ten years ago and involved restructuring the human resource policy for the whole plant, which in those days was a huge assignment for me. I was surprised that he used consultants for the work; there was so much talent in his own organization. But actually that's why he brought consultants in, to more or less overcome any possible resistance to restructuring, which in a talented organization could be something to contend with. He was absolutely clear about what had to happen, a good sport, and a pleasure to work with.

GEERT VAN DEE

Everybody Was Envious

I've worked for 200 clients at least, and in almost every possible industry. And a major men's magazine was one of those. The man who started it was legendary—I never met him because he spent all of his time in his bedroom. He didn't know what was going on in the office because he spent all of his time editing the text and airbrushing the photographs But that was very good a client, mostly because everybody in the Cresap, McCormick, Paget office was envious of me.

RAY EPICH

No Bad Clients

Overall, I don't think that I've had any real bad clients. All my clients have always paid their bills. I mean even the worst guy in the world, you work with them, so to speak. You try to get them to see things your way and to depend on you.

STEVE GOLDFIELD

A Vision of Something Big

I think a good client is a challenging client, one with a direction and a vision of something big. A good client would like to accomplish something and demands excellence.

Clients who have the consultants around because of politics, or try to leverage the consultants to cause things to happen that are in the individual's interests as opposed to the company's interest—those are bad clients.

ANONYMOUS B

DILBERT: © Scott Adams/Dist. By United Feature Syndicate, Inc.

He Put the A-Team On It

As a consultant, you look for signs of leadership. The toughest engagement is when someone brings us in and says, go help this guy who works for me and the guy is doing the project only because he's afraid not to. He doesn't really want to do the project. That's when things get tough.

For example, my partner recently called me to express concern about a potential project with a finance company. The company had told us they wanted to do the project. But we we're having a hard time getting through to the chairman. We made it clear we wouldn't do this until we met with the chairman. My partner was concerned that because he was having such a hard time getting through, the chairman was probably not going to show much commitment.

Well, we finally did meet with him and actually it turned out wonderfully. He told us, "Listen, I'm putting my A-team on this project." My partner was in and out of there in 40 minutes, for a $1.2 million deal. That's what I mean by leadership. He put the A-team on it and sent a message to the company that we're serious about this. What a difference that makes. But we had to wait for that sign of commitment.

I can relate one other experience with a bank where the head of operations and systems had brought us in, and a senior vice president didn't want us there. Before we even got there, he was cutting every tree he could to block our path. I said to their operations head, "We'll try to work with this guy. It's going to be difficult, but we'll work with him. We'll try and convert him." So he arranged for me have lunch with the vice chairman of the bank. At the lunch the vice-chairman asked me what was going to be the biggest obstacle? I told him, your senior vice president of operations doesn't want us here. His only response was, "Okay, anything else?"

Well, two weeks later we showed up on a Monday to start the job, and this senior VP was gone. They had fired him! The vice chairman said this project was too important to have one person get in the way of our success. Frankly, in my opinion, this guy had cut his own throat. I mean, he was irrational, claiming there couldn't be anything wrong with his operating area. That was just stupid. He should have just said yes, I can use the help. We would have made a hero out of him.

We gained so much from their willingness to not let him interfere. About halfway through the project we found ourselves eight or nine weeks ahead of schedule, so I told them we would, if they liked, do the corporate loan division for free. This had not been part of the original agreement. But they had done us a great favor by removing the leadership obstacle we faced. They had shown leadership and integrity. Consequently, I felt it was appropriate that we reciprocate.

CARL LOBUE

A Friend and a Partner

When people say, put it in the contract, write it down so we know you're go-ing to deliver this, this, this and this, it's like you're just another supplier. But a great client doesn't make you a supplier. A great client makes you a friend and partner in the effort. And you just can't imagine disappointing them. That's when consulting is at its best. It becomes about friendship and trust.

BILL MATASSONI

A Big Budget

The criteria can evolve over time, but a good client is definitely one with a big budget.

JAMES BLOMBERG

DEFINING THE BAD CLIENT

Essentially Fraud

If you've worked in this business, there are always stories. I once worked for the CIO of a major client and got into a situation where he was trying to pressure me to use another firm as a subcontractor. Suddenly, I was getting bills for work that wasn't performed. So I went to this guy and said, okay, you sign this bill and I'll pay it. He wouldn't sign it. And that proved to be the end of our relationship.

We got rid of the subcontractor and lo and behold we were fired. And that was fine with me. Later, this fellow was fired for what was essentially fraud. I'm not sure how the money passed from the subcontractor to him, but it was clear to me at the time that we were in the middle of something we didn't want to be involved in. This was actually a Fortune 500 company. But you don't see much of that.

ANONYMOUS B

Doesn't Take Ownership

I think a bad client is one that brings you in without the right preparation and the right mindset on his or her part. It's a client that says it's the consultants' project, and doesn't take ownership of it. It's a client that doesn't have again the fortitude and the will to really do the things that are necessary to make lasting change really happen.

LANNY COHEN

Only Addressing 30 Percent of the Problems

Sometimes we would get hired because the contact's archenemy somewhere else in the company had some project going. We would get hired so they had something to say at the next meeting. And while we were there to solve an issue, because of the way we were hired, we were only addressing 30 percent of the problems instead of 50 percent of the problems or 100 percent of the problems.

There are times, too, when you get hired because they don't have enough courage. To put it more nicely, when you're working with utilities, a lot of times you're working with companies that have been true monopolies in the past, and it's hard for them to make decisions that would impact their friends and their neighbors and a lot of times their relatives. So we would get hired to come in and make those hard choices for them. Sometimes this was obvious, but that's what we would do. With some clients we made a material difference. But with others even though they spent all that money, nothing came of it. Not because the work we did wasn't of high quality, but they didn't have any way to take that work and incorporate it into the business. The organizations were too large, or they didn't have direction or leadership.

JAMES BLOMBERG

You Will Cooperate!

I had a situation where I was working for a client, and we talked to the client about our approach, the methodology we were going to use, whom we had to interview and that sort of thing. We underscored the importance of cooperation from middle management. So we helped the client script his opening speech to the middle management team. The script was to say that this was an important project for the organization, and that we need your cooperation and value your input, and we need for you to work with the consultants and support them in what they're trying to do.

Now, this guy was a real hard-driving type of executive. He got middle management in a room. He started off okay, talking about how important the project was, but pretty soon his real personality came out. He starts talking about how you will cooperate and the first time I see somebody not cooperating, they're fired. Not in so many words, but that's practically what he said. We just wanted to crawl under the chair. Now this is the environment under which we had to start working with these people.

So obviously they're going to tell us everything we need to know, right? So, I had to circle the wagons. I had to go back and say, "Hey look, if you do that again, we're out of here, because it isn't going to work." And then I had to really use those relationship skills, to be able to sit down with these middle managers and say, "What the CEO really meant to say was this, not that." Fortunately, in that situation, everybody knew the CEO and knew his style. I think if he had done it any other way, they probably would have had more problems with that, thinking he was really spewing the BS then, because there's no way he ever normally talked like that.

LANNY COHEN

Not Prepared

A bad client is a situation where the client's organization is not prepared to handle a job. They cannot carry out your recommendations successfully. You usually pick up on it pretty early. You sense the opportunities for success are not there, that you'd almost be better off not to take the assignment. Certainly in our experience we've had to give up on assignments, rather than continuing on something where there seemed little chance of really helping. I'm just talking about a basic failure on the part of the client's organization to respond to the help you're trying to give them.

ROBERT HAMMAN

Inaccessible

A bad client is one who is inaccessible. One who doesn't want to sit down with the consultant during the course of a project to discuss where things are going, what the findings are leading toward. As I said, this can be important because if there is a disconnect of some kind during the project, clients can help fix it before it gets too deep. They can also help navigate the political waters of their organization for the buy-in that's needed to make change really happen.

WAYNE COOPER

Hunger Spoiled Our Judgment

There have been a lot of low points but the lowest was an occasion where I think we let hunger spoil our judgment. We were hired by a major brokerage firm that no longer exists. Plenty has been written about its demise. The CEO had gotten them into serious trouble, basically through a real estate investment to build a big building for headquarters. It was just insane. I mean, the whole top floor was going to be a huge office for him. He was basically tanking the company.

"While you were out, sir, the company, rudderless and adrift, operated pretty much the same as always."

We were brought in after the fact to help decide on how to move certain operations to a lower cost environment so they could lease out additional space to help pay for the building. This required getting consensus from a lot of people in the organization. All the pieces of the company were very interrelated, so it was a matter of getting agreement on what parts could be operated at a distance without dropping the company in the process.

There was a new president who had been brought in from another large brokerage firm who was very highly regarded, but who ultimately failed at getting his arms around this situation. So he was canned. Part of the problem was every department operated as a little fiefdom and these guys hated each other and guarded their turf relentlessly. Basically, the concept of consensus didn't exist in this organization.

The CEO was also deliberately undercutting every decision the new president made. So then here we came marching into an environment where the person who had real power was trying to undercut everything we did, and it was very unpleasant. We also failed. That was one low point. If we had been wiser and less hungry, we never would have taken the work.

FORD HARDING

Get Out of Government Consulting

After trying to build our state government practice, I eventually made the decision to get out of government consulting. Over the years I had come to find it a very frustrating market. There are so many regulatory requirements to deal with, a lot of bureaucracy. It is basically a bid business. There isn't the same urgency or focus on driving for a result that you normally find in the commercial markets. There isn't the sense of being held accountable for bottom-line results.

Of course, there are also the political considerations, which are different from the usual corporate politics. It's a different thing when people are worried about being in the press, worried about the public response. I remember a dispute we got into with one government agency over the scope of the work and the contract and other issues. There was a very tense meeting with the head of this agency, who said to us, in so many words, "By God, if you don't agree to our terms, I'm going to call the press and tomorrow it will be all over the front pages how your firm caused problems for this state." I told him, "If that's what you need to do, then so be it." But I also told him how we looked at it. How some of what they wanted was out of our scope. And we were not going to do the work unless we could agree on a contract amendment.

Ultimately, I've come to the conclusion that the public sector is a very large market but also a very frustrating market. Our firm decided we just weren't going to pursue that market.

DAVID TIERNO

RATING THE CLIENT

Just Move On

A difficult client would be someone who calls you in, but who really doesn't want to be working with you. I happen to like the saying, "Never do business with someone you don't want to do business with." Quite right, categorically. When you're successful enough to work that way, that's absolutely right. You just move on. Next.

ELIZABETH KOVACS

Use You as an Alibi

The only major problem with clients is when they use you as an alibi for their own problems. It can be very difficult to work with that type of client. A client who is uncertain or hesitant or just using you as an alibi, that is tough.

GEERT VAN DEE

Can't Get Beyond Your Skin Color

As far as low points go, one was a study I did for an East Coast state in 1988. It was a report on the issue of whether the state lottery exploits the poor. I gave some outstanding research evidence that it does. As a result, I was treated like crap and blocked from future business. After that I stopped doing business with all state government agencies. Frankly, I think they thought with an issue like this that only white researchers could do an objective analysis. But I had gone into all different types of poor neighborhoods, not just black, but Latino, white, Native American, all across my home state. The results were very representative of the population.

This was a low point because you want to believe as a researcher that you're doing the best job possible, and that people trust that. But when people can't get beyond your skin color, it's a real problem. Unfortunately, that still exists today. I mean, it's lessening but it's still there. Interestingly, they found out later the recommendations I had made were right. It was just in the local newspapers, ten years later. It's also been shown that the monies were not distributed as originally designed. More lottery money in our home state is going for prisons, rather than for schools and the elderly, which is what the law originally mandated. So now it's becoming a little controversial.

ALISON JACKSON

Report Stayed On the Shelf

Only a few times over the last 25 years can I say a report stayed on the shelf. Usually you know if that's going to happen within the first week of the project. More often than not it's because of some political struggle that's taking place, as opposed to anything in the content of the report.

ALAN ANDOLSEN

I Don't Need You

I can remember one example. Our client was a charitable organization best known for plaques and work in schools. The president was ineffective and had a lot of problems. We were asked to reorganize the place.

They then brought in a retired army general. He took over and we had our first progress report. And I'll never forget it, I was so very young then. It is stuff from your early career that you remember to most vividly. The general looked at me and said, "I ran the (bleeping) U.S. Army and you're telling me that I can't run this (bleeping) candy store. That I need you?" I guess I knew I was in trouble right then.

Well, there was dead silence, the partners just kind of blended in with the woodwork. I said, "Sir, I guess that our assignment is over, isn't it?" "You betcha it is," he said.

ED PRINGLE

-4-

Managing Client Relationships

"Being a professional involves looking after the client's best interests."

FORD HARDING

onsultants are hired to solve problems, develop strategies, overcome hurdles, and meet goals. Accordingly, most consulting projects will be judged by the success or failure of their strategic or financial objectives. Solve the problem!

But on another level, success as a consultant hinges on how much mutual integrity, trust, communication and understanding are brought to the business relationship. In other words, what kind of bond or connection has been established between a consultant and a client?

How do you build relationships with clients? By definition consulting is a client-centric business. That means a relationship-oriented business. The best consultants and firms never forget this. They have an outward focus on the market and on clients. They go to bed thinking about their clients and they get up in the morning thinking about their clients. What more can we do? How can we serve them better? How do we get them to like us better? Where did we go wrong? How can we make it up? Have we anticipated all their needs? The plots and counterplots. If we follow this course, will the client love us more? It's all about clients, period.

How do you deal with the challenges involved in telling clients what they need to hear, when it is not necessarily what they want to hear? How do you bring expertise to the table without appearing arrogant or bruising egos? Most clients want answers, not process, and have little interest in watching a room full of background research unfurled before them. The best consultants take the long view on their work, understanding when to get out of a project or association, sacrificing short-term income for long-term credibility.

There's some consultant folk wisdom here, too. Like, never give your client a nickname, because it just might slip out....

Consulting Was Always About Clients

Some consulting firms emphasize their products, while others focus on their staff. Obviously both are important. But to me, the business of consulting was always about clients and the building of relationships with those clients. Our end products often are nebulous, and the client must have a strong feeling of trust in the consultant to allow him into his business, to create major changes, and to pay him the big dollars.

I went to Little Rock, Arkansas, for the first time in 1976. Arkansas Power & Light Company asked us to carry out a company-wide management and operations review. The company was part of Middle South Utilities (later Entergy Corporation), a utility holding company with subsidiaries in Louisiana, Mississippi and later Texas.

I commuted from Chicago to Little Rock every Monday morning through Friday night for close to two years. During that time, I believe I met the entire management team, and visited most of their offices throughout the state (Toad Suck Ferry is my personal favorite name for an Arkansas town). I had dinner with their directors several times and was invited into the homes of a great many of the key players in the company. I really enjoyed working with the Arkansans and still keep up to date with several of them 25 years later.

Ultimately, six of the managers and officers that I worked with became presidents and CEO's of other utilities. Think about that, a smallish utility in Arkansas being the cradle for that many top people. And other managers moved up the ladder at Middle South and at other utilities even though they may not have reached the top spot. And guess what, old Metzler went with them throughout their careers. I had project work at one of the Middle South companies every year for at least the next 20 years. And I followed the others as they went to their new positions at other utilities in Texas, North Carolina, Georgia, Pennsylvania, Tennessee and New Jersey. Literally, I developed a major business out of one client early in my career as a consultant.

By the way, when I started my own shop in 1984, I first went to see one of the six managers who later became a president of a utility, in this case Arkansas Power & Light Company. I told him that I was thinking about starting my own business. Without blinking an eye, he said that was a great idea and that he wanted to be my first client. He gave me a two-year retainer that was enough to pay the mortgage and the car payments and to keep food on the table. By the end of the first year, I had another six consultants working on my projects throughout the utility industry and I was on my way to building a major firm.

RICHARD METZLER

Can You Fix the Car Too Well?

Is there a fine line between being the perfect consultant and being a really good consultant? Can you fix the car too well? For me, the answer to that is easy. You always fix the car perfectly. You always do your assignment to the best of your ability. But you can't fix an organization perfectly. The guy will at some point have to buy a new car. So you can only do what you think is right at the moment. But you never, ever, ever try to wire yourself in. It's a mistake that even some of the best consultants make. I mean, there's so much they can do. But the corporation needs them so much they could just be there forever. Have fifteen engagements going on at once, millions of dollars a month in billing, thirty, forty, fifty people at the client site.

Well, sooner or later the client gets sick of you. The really good consultants understand that they should fix things and get out. They even understand that they should sometimes not fix things and get out. The wrong answer is not to fix things so you can stay in. The client will ask you to return, but if they don't that's fine because there will be other clients out there. That's probably the line that separates ordinary senior consultants from truly outstanding senior consultants. The outstanding ones will have a sense of when to leave the client alone and enough confidence in their capability to build new relationships and move on.

BILL MATASSONI

Are You Still Driving That Cadillac?

I was working on a major project in Toronto and had arrived very late one night at the airport. It was the last flight in, actually. I went to the rental car agency where the person there was very happy to tell me that because it was so late and they only had one car left, they were going to give me a free upgrade to a luxury car. I said that was nice, but no, I didn't want a luxury car. Well, actually, that was all they had left. I decided to check first with the other agencies, but most had closed and the ones still open had no cars left. So I ended up back at the first agency, driving out in a brand new Cadillac.

The next morning I decided it was probably not a good thing to park a new Cadillac in the client's parking lot. I parked way across the street. Made it through the day fine. At the end of the day, the vice president happened to be leaving as I was, and saw me crossing the street and getting into this Cadillac. Do you know I worked for that client and that VP for the next two years, and later, this same VP moved to another company and I worked with him there, too. And for the next five years, every time that fellow saw me, his first question would be, "Are you still driving that Cadillac?" It did not matter how much I explained the situation– that it was rented at the same rate you would have paid for a Ford Taurus. It didn't matter. It was the image that counted. He didn't want consultants coming to his plant driving Cadillacs.

COBY FRAMPTON

Looking After the Client's Best Interests

I remember one client we worked for that had terrible labor-management relations. The company had hired a cost-cutting consulting firm to come in and that consultant was paid on the basis of the amount of savings their work would generate. So they came in with an ax and started chopping. In the short run, they saved the company a lot of money. But in the process they so alienated labor from management that the company never really did recover. They ended up just short of bankruptcy.

I'm sure they thought they were doing a good job. Yet it was very short-sighted. They lost track of what the company was trying to do, which ultimately was to be a successful, profitable organization. Instead, they just focused on the job they'd been assigned to do, which was to find cash now. And in the process they caused great harm.

The client also has some responsibility. These are not naive buyers in most cases. They're sophisticated business people in their own right. So the blame certainly extends to the client, too. But that does not mean that consultant should have done what he did. Of course, I imagine there are cases where clients also have protected us from ourselves.

Part of being a professional involves looking after the client's best interests. In reality, you often have technical expertise and specialized knowledge that the client doesn't have. You may understand the implications of decisions better than the client can. But there's also a delicate line you don't want to cross, where you start to come across as arrogant and presumptuous because you think you understand the client's interest.

If a client is acting on self-serving motives, I think that makes it easier for consultants to come in and run amok. I'm talking about individuals who want things done for very selfish reasons that have nothing to do with the good of the company. Or they've forgotten that the company, in most cases, does not belong to them.

FORD HARDING

The Link to People

I try to caution my partners not to fall into the thinking, no matter how confident they may be in their advice, that there is really only one correct solution. If I, for example, told six people where I live and said meet me there in two hours, I'm sure those six would all get there. But they might also take six different routes. One person might take the absolutely wrong route and arrive very late. Another might get there a little earlier than everyone else, while the rest might arrive in more or less the same time.

Of course, none of those five would be exclusively wrong or right in the route they took. That's how it is in our profession. There are often multiple solutions to any situation. The pitfall we need to avoid is to believe our solution is the only solution, or that there is only one correct solution. It's important in our business not to get too cocky.

In my estimation, the consultants who really try to understand the client's business and concerns make the best consultants. They are the ones who recognize what I call the link to people. Remember when everyone was talking about reengineering? That was the buzzword for a long time. Well, most of us in this business have been doing reengineering and process improvement all of our professional lives. Back in the days when I was doing brokerage work at Andersen Consulting, that is what we were doing. We just didn't call it that. So I've learned that you can reorganize processes all you want, but if you exclude the people factor, you're in trouble; because it is the people in an organization who have to implement change.

Those in our profession who recognize the people factor in its totality have the best chance at success. In many cases, the solution that we think objectively to be the optimal solution may not necessarily or always be so. That's because it may not work in the client's particular environment or culture.

WILLARD ARCHIE

"Try as we might, sir, our team of managment consultants has been unable to find a single fault in the manner in which you conduct your business. Everything you do is a hundred per cent right. Keep it up! That will be eleven thousand dollars."

Creating a Story, Not Finding the Holy Grail

In a sense, consulting is about creating a story, not finding the Holy Grail. We spend a lot of time coming up with information, doing research, and then working with the information. It's all about taking a set of facts, figures, and events and creating a theme around them. When we do a presentation we're taking that story or theme and leading the client through it to an acceptable or perhaps even exciting conclusion. This is what clients expect.

How can I best say it? Perhaps clients expect to hear the buzz words. But what you have to do is create an entire plot around those words. In a sense, you're setting up a burning platform and telling the client they had better do something about it. They can either jump off that platform or they can reconstruct it, but they need to do something different. It is then up to us to outline all the options and try to draw out their implications.

Actually, I think the intellectual aspect of our work might be a little overblown. I don't think there's as much brainstorming and trying to find the next great idea as much as there is just taking existing ideas and trying to wrap it up in a new package. Apply it in a new context. In reality most of our time is spent on fairly mundane matters. We probably put about 50 percent of our time into research and 20 to 30 percent of our time is in meetings with clients. There are always a lot of meetings. The other 20 percent of the time is sort of the fill-in kind of stuff, whether it's traveling, making phone calls, or dealing with internal, administrative types of issues. I probably spend over half of my time by myself, doing research.

Of course, you do have to be a smart person to do well in this business. But you also have to be very people savvy. You have to understand how to get along with all sorts of people. If you're really smart but don't understand the people side of things, you're not going to do well. It also goes without saying that you can be very people savvy, but if the intellectual content is lacking, you're not going to do well, either.

STEVE GOLDFIELD

MANAGING CLIENT RELATIONSHIPS

A Partnership With Clients

I like to talk about a partnership with clients. It's the attitude that we're solving problems together. They're not asking us to give them a solution; we're working as a team. There's a mutual recognition that both sides need to be flexible in the way we approach things. Consulting becomes something you're doing with clients, rather than to clients. And the clients understand that and desire that. If you can really develop what for lack of a better word I would call a relationship with the client, then you're going to be much better off than if you're viewed as strictly a vendor.

MICHAEL LAPORTA

Ambivalence to the Relationship

Some consultants are very good. Some are fair. Some are no good at all. But most of them I believe are pretty good. They really do know how to help. They have particular professional skills to help the client. In my experience, I would say where consultants fail most is in the subjective part of the relationship. Ninety-nine percent of all consultants give all their attention to what I call "the objective reality," meaning how to help the client solve a particular problem. It's not that they don't help the client to solve the problem. But they pay no attention at all to the personal quality of the client relationship.

Here's what I mean. Suppose you asked for advice and I started criticizing you. Let's assume that the criticism was really good and insightful. How are you going to feel? You're going to resent it like hell. You're going to say that I don't know what I'm talking about, or you're going to feel stupid—why didn't I think of that, he must be smarter than I am? And so it's a no-win situation.

Assuming it was good advice, the client is going to resent the fact that I thought of something that he didn't. Also, he's going to feel dependent upon me because I gave him an answer to a problem that he didn't have. So there's ambivalence to the relationship. There's both the respect and an appreciation for the help I'm giving him and there's a resentment that he had to come to me to get it. I think this is at the heart of the problems that arise in consulting relationships.

So what's the solution to this? I think first and foremost the answer for me is to be terribly aware of how the client is going to feel if I give him the "right" answer. Secondly, I need to be aware that my client is absolutely no different from me. He doesn't like to be criticized. We're all that way. The dilemma is that on the one hand, if I don't tell him the absolute truth, I have no value. I'm a phony. But on the other hand, if I do tell him the truth, I have got to find a way to let him save face. I have got to find a way to let him psychologically accept the criticism I'm giving him. That's where most consultants fail.

I want the client to see that I'm not being judgmental, I'm not condemning him. I'm saying, we're all human and we all make mistakes. Then he will find it acceptable to listen to what I have to say.

So whenever my partners and I would go into a client situation, we would always look at the problem on two levels. One was the objective level—what's the best way to help solve the problem? But the other hand, we pay almost as much attention to the subjective level, meaning how are we going to make what we say psychologically acceptable to the client?

CHESTER BURGER

Form a Bond and that Makes a Difference

When you have some kind of bond with a client, this also really helps. With some long-term clients, you form a bond and that makes a difference. For example, I had occasion to meet recently with a client who had just been promoted within a large corporation. He is in a new position now, with a company he's worked at for over 15 years. So we were catching up to see where things were at, in regard to possibilities for future work. This is the kind of client who is always nearby.

Let me tell you a little about how we go back. He is from the southeast and truly a good old boy. He had been manager of a plant in Alabama and the company transferred him to Green Bay, Wisconsin. He hadn't been there too long when he asked me to come up to work on a project. So I paid him a visit up there in Green Bay. A winter visit, I should say. Well, the day I was there the assistant plant manager came in about noon and said he thought they'd better send everybody home because the weather was getting bad. As it turned out they ended up shutting the plant down. The only two people left there were me and this fellow, two guys from the southeast. We stuck it out for the afternoon.

That night, it finally cleared up, at least enough for us to drive to a local restaurant. The airport was still closed. During dinner I made a remark about how you always hear about how people from the south can't handle the bad weather. A little snow falls and we all panic and close our airports and shut down our plants; how people from the north harass us about this. Yet here we were, two guys from the southeast and the only ones in the restaurant, the only ones willing to go out in this weather. You know, it was kind of a bonding experience. It was a chance for the two of us to really sit down and talk. We probably spent about six hours together, and I learned more about him and his background, his company's way of doing business. It helps you in the future.

COBY FRAMPTON

They Want Answers, Not Process

In the early days of my work, and perhaps to some extent even lingering today, there is this internal pressure you feel that you have to surprise the client. To feel that you have to provide the client with something that is very high level. But the discovery I've made over the years is that the client really wants basics, not exotica. They want answers, not process. They want babies, not to hear about the birth pains. The client doesn't want you to render up all the data you may have created, and call that part of the report. The client, especially in the construction industry, is entrepreneurial driven, results focused. And, while we may take elaborate steps to get to a conclusion, elaborating those steps does not impress the client. What impresses the client is speed, accuracy, and preferably low cost.

Of course, you can't always give them all three. But if you have focused recommendations, well, that's what it is all about. I'm not saying that data isn't important. It is. But as a backdrop that's usually best left in the briefcase. If clients want to see data, then you can show them more. But packaging some 30-pound report is not useful. On several occasions, I've seen clients get upset with consultants. They felt they were given a product that was mostly BS. Their directive was to cut the BS and focus on the useful part.

When something like that happens, I really just try to take it as a reminder. Client satisfaction is number one. That's why we've been doing formal client evaluations of our work for years. Looking at our approach, the degree of communication, all the factors that go into a job well done. I can admit there have been a couple of times when I've forgotten some of these things.

JERRY JACKSON

Defuse Problems With Clients' Employees

There are a handful of ways to defuse problems with clients' employees. The first and most important way is that the senior management and leadership of the company have to be engaged and be visible. They have to really sponsor the project! The company has to be willing to work at it. If a company thinks the consultant is going to defuse all the problems, you'd better not embark on this thing in the first place because that's the wrong use of your consultants. Although certainly the consultants can help, we can help communicate. We'll coach executives in terms of how to deal with conflict, those types of situations. Obviously, too, our behavior as consultants can affect the situation. I don't want to absolve consultants in our industry of their behavior because there are plenty of consultants out there who can go in and find more ways to upset an organization, and end up putting an organization at a disadvantage.

So, although our job isn't necessarily to defuse every situation, it surely also isn't to create problems, either. Just by the very nature of coming in the door and being who we are, you've got to be cautious of that. But it's hard to defuse. The way we coach and train our people for these situations is to focus on relationships early on. You have to build relationships with the right people, both junior and senior people, right away so they can come to you and almost be the safety valve to let you know about conflict early on. And then you can work through the organization to defuse the conflict.

That becomes a very important strategic aspect of what we do during these transformations, because everything comes down to very personal issues in the end. It doesn't mean conflicts are solved every time, and it doesn't mean these problems don't happen. But I think the best way to defuse conflicts is through a combination of forming good relationships and making sure our client's senior management does its job.

I have no problem telling a CEO, "Here's what you have to do. You want to do this project, you want to hire us, and you're investing a boatload of money to do this. Here's your job. Here are the ten things that you have to do to make this thing go." And we'll have very frank conversations. "Unless you're prepared to do it, don't begin because you're not going to get there. It's going to be a huge failure. You, yourself, will be embarrassed. The Board will have your shoes," and so on and so forth. But if the CEO is willing to do what it takes, that becomes the first critical success factor in a major improvement program. You can see that factor when the project works, and when the project doesn't work, it's not there. It's one of those things that is so obvious.

LANNY COHEN

No Presumptive Sell

There's no such thing as the presumptive sell in our line of work. That's one of the realities I've learned in working with clients. You can't walk in and convince anybody. But if you know they have a serious problem and they're aware of it, the deal is closed in no time. I mean, it's just how fast can you get in here and help us? I've been working with a financial services company whose CEO literally had a one-day turnaround to give the go-ahead on a major project. I went in and here it was, here's what we want to do. I sent him our proposal in a fax and he was practically calling me before the fax was finished. When can we get started? That's very unusual. At that level, they've usually delegated it to somebody.

ALAN ANDOLSEN

An Even Bigger Reward In the Long-term

One definition of maturity is the ability to defer an immediate reward for an even bigger reward in the long-term. My firm had been retained by Texas Utilities to provide regulatory support to management and to their attorneys during a rate case involving the Comanche Peak Nuclear Plant. The case and the hearings dragged on for years. We had a team in place throughout that time. At first, we played a key role in setting the strategy and assembling the overall rate case team. Eventually, however, the effort centered on the attorneys and the witnesses and our role was reduced to ready standby in the event that something popped up that had to be taken care of right away. Although this was very profitable, it wasn't very satisfying and it certainly didn't serve the client in the best possible way.

Finally, I went to the president, and told him that I thought it was time for our involvement to come to an end. He was paying us for work that wasn't needed. We would be available if something came up, but it was time for us to leave. In case you think that I was losing my grip, I should mention as an aside that our firm had plenty of other work and that we could reassign the staff to other clients and other projects by the next week.

But Texas Utilities saw us as the only consulting firm that ever volunteered to leave a project, to do what was best for the client even though it cost us money. My reputation was made at Texas Utilities. The president and I became very close friends and we still are. He is a very bright guy and has a wonderful sense of humor. Very often we would literally know what the other was thinking.

Over the years, Texas Utilities became one of my largest clients. And they always referred to me and the firm as the "honest consultants."

RICHARD METZLER

You Can't Just Kiss Up

You can't just kiss up to the majority shareholders. That's never the right approach. Over time, the failure to do the right stuff will find a way to bite you back. You always have to look at the bigger picture, at the things that need fixing. The client will go bankrupt if you're too much of a wuss to give the right recommendation, or too ineffective as a salesperson to promote your idea and get them to take action on it. Also, if you think your work is done the moment you've made a recommendation, that's wrong too.

JERRY JACKSON

Peanuts: © United Feature Syndicate, Inc.

A Strong Balance Sheet Gives You Moral Courage

I think one of the age-old problems of consulting is whether you slant your recommendations one way or another in order to have a continuing relationship with the client. We recognize that clients have a propensity to like one answer better than the other, and that if you keep feeding up answers they don't like, no matter how truthful they may be, you've probably shortened your time with the client.

Well, that's led me to a couple of conclusions. You can talk about how to broach recommendations you know are going to be unpopular. But perhaps what is more important is your own firm's position. Consulting firms typically look at their profit and loss statement, but I think it's important that you manage the firm by its balance sheet. And by that I mean to always have a strong balance sheet, a strong net worth and plenty of liquidity. Because if you've got a solid balance sheet, then you can always tell the client what he needs to hear rather than what he wants to hear. We're all human. If we're living at the edge of survival and barely able to pay our bills, it is only human that the often subtle distinction between what the client needs to hear and what the client wants to hear gets fuzzed over. And I found that having a strong balance sheet gives you the moral courage to earn your living properly as a consultant. What I mean by that is to tell the client what they need to hear rather than what they want to hear, but also do it in a way that doesn't blow your relationship because then you've lost your opportunity to have an impact.

CARL SLOANE

A Job Offer

Every consulting assignment in its own right has got a little romance in it in terms of the client relationship. Thirty years ago, one of the ways you knew whether you were successful or not on engagements was whether you got a job offer. It was definitely a measuring stick then, but I don't think it is today. Younger consultants should know that used to be a way to judge success.

Now, whether you should take the job offer is a whole different subject. I had an offer about 20 years ago for probably five times what I was making at the time. It was an extraordinary money offer, but it was an iffy situation. I thought it through, and realized that the chairman of this company wanted me to come and be his chief operating officer, because he had a huge problem he wanted me to fix. I wondered what my half-life would be once the problem was fixed, because it was a fixable problem.

So here this guy was, spending a lot of money on me and the consulting team to do this work. I imagine he just did a simple little cost benefit analysis: He's thinking, let's say I'll hire this guy for a lot more than he's making. He won't be able to resist the temptation. He'll fix the problem and in a couple of years I can get rid of him. Perhaps the lesson was, even if they offer you five times your income, you better think through what it's really about.

ANONYMOUS A

Something On the Floor to Make Noise

Managing relationships means having to adapt to all kind of personalities or management styles. We consulted to the utility industry where some of the firms in the industry had the reputation of being somewhat slow moving. At least this was true before deregulation. Somewhat after, too, for that matter.

We had a Southern client, a section manager at one of the major utilities. He was a grand old Southern gentleman with a great accent. He was section manager at this really labyrinthine organization, and we suspected he probably didn't have to work that hard to earn his keep.

He had this corner office, with a great view outside. The office was U-shaped, and when you came into the office, you saw a couch and his actual desk was around the corner out of view.

And what he would do is he would sit up at his desk with his head resting on his hands and his feet up on the desk. He had a very tiny mirror the size of a three-by-five card planted on the back of the couch. And he had something on the floor that would make noise when you walked in. So with the noise, he could look up and see you in the mirror. He'd turn around to his credenza to compose himself, and then he'd swing around to face you.

I thought that was just a remarkable way to go about business. The entire organization knew of it and that's just how he did things. We were told that's just what he does.

JAMES BLOMBERG

Don't Y'all Ever Finish Another Man's Sentence

I had never been south of the Mason-Dixon Line when I got a call to go to Little Rock, Arkansas. The client was Arkansas Power & Light Company, and we were asked to carry out a company-wide audit of management and operations.

Their Senior Vice President was a gentleman in his 60's, just a few years from retirement. He would start most conversations by pulling out a pipe, loading it with tobacco, firing it up, blowing smoke rings and looking at ceilings. Sometimes he would put the pipe in the pocket of his old tweed sport coat and smoke would come out of his pocket. He was very calm and deliberate, the essence of southern courtesy in every way. In contrast, at that time I was a young Yankee. Brusque, fast talking, in a hurry, always pushing as hard as I could. He and I were almost complete opposites.

One day, he asked me stop by and chat. He started out with his pipe, of course. He told me that I probably had some promise and looked to him like a decent guy, and that he would like me to succeed with our work at the company. But he had three bits of advice for me. I don't even remember the first two suggestions but I sure remember the third. Because when he got to his third point, he stopped and went through his pipe routine. And this time, he took even longer than usual. In my inimitable fashion, I said, "Is it this?" "Is it that?" "Could this be what you mean?" "Have we talked about this?" And on and on.

Finally, I ran out of ideas and stopped talking. He took some more time and relit his pipe. He then looked over and slowly said, "Metzler, don't y'all ever finish another man's sentence."

Ouch! I never ever forgot that bit of advice.

RICHARD METZLER

Keep In Touch

We keep in touch. For example, with a major beverage company back in the '70s we set up their first records management system. In the late '80s, companies were moving into digital systems. We wanted to do that in the '70s but the company's IT group was not ready then. You'd think it was a little weird that a company that size hadn't gotten its act together. But by the end of the '80s it had, and we said, okay, it's time, let's do it. We'd stayed in touch so we could do that. Most of us have had relationships like that, over long periods of time.

In one case, we had a client whom we had worked for in '51 or '52 and they called us back around '86 or '87. This was a government client. We also stay in touch through connections we have in professional associations. We'll see people on either an annual or semi-annual basis. If we're doing a presentation, we might have people who we've worked with come up and say, "Hey, you know, that sparks something. Maybe we need to talk to you about this. Let's get together." But it's follow-up work and is never of the same magnitude as the initial project.

All of our focus is on practical, day-to-day issues, so whether they're staying up to date usually becomes real obvious to the client. They know when they're having a problem. A few of the clients, usually the smaller ones, want to retain us as a sort of quality check for them. It's usually because it's only part time for someone there to make sure things are going okay. In these situations, they want us to come back and diagnose it from outside. To say, is it still healthy? Or do we need to be doing some other things?

ALAN ANDOLSEN

You Are Known By Clients You Serve

The strength of McKinsey over the years was in their client selection. It goes back to the brand issue. For example, there's some mythology at McKinsey about Marvin Bowers being asked to consult for General Motors. The story goes that Marvin had said, in response, "That's fine, but I really need to clear this with your chairman. We work only with the very top and I want his commitment on this." The fellow he was working with said, "Look, I'm a senior guy here. I give you my word. But if you want I'll bring in the vice-chairman of the board." So the vice-chairman comes in and reaffirms how really committed they are to working with McKinsey. Again, Marvin says, "Fine, I really appreciate it. But I still want to talk to the chairman." So finally they brought the chairman in.

Now whether it really happened exactly that way, I've got no idea. But the mythology was that you've got to have great clients and they have to be running the company. Or be in a position to make tough decisions and get people to act. The broader lesson is that you are only as good as your clients. If you pick bad clients or if you tolerate bad clients or you tolerate their definition of the problem, that will not enable you to serve them properly. You're dead then.

I think over the years McKinsey has made better decisions about their clients than other consulting firms for two reasons. One, it was drilled into the senior guys by Marvin and other leaders of the firm. Second, when you're on top and reasonably busy it's much easier to say no. You know the Moll Flanders story, give me food lest I steal. Well, it's a reinforcing cycle. If you can say no, people respect you. You've got to be willing to walk away. Basically, you are known by the clients you serve, and your work as a consultant is entirely affected by their ability to make things happen.

BILL MATASSONI

You Can't Negotiate If You're Backing Up

If you have a really bad client, you should resign or they should fire you. You ought to make it uncomfortable enough that you get fired. I've been fired by a really great client who, at the time, was really pissed at some actions that we were taking. This was a more than a $20 million relationship. This was a big, big client, it was a culmination of some scope change issues, and I just didn't make it happen. You can't negotiate if you're backing up all the time.

So he fired me. I said, "Are you sure you want to do this?" His response was, expletive, expletive, expletive, you're outta here. I told him I felt very bad that we had reached this conclusion, because I think we've made a lot of progress together. But he basically threw me out of his office; he would not shake hands with me.

Now his chairman learned of this and thought through the consequences and basically reversed the decision to eliminate us as a firm. But I was definitely history. Roll the clock forward a year. I get a phone call from this guy. He says "I know we had a problem a year ago. A lot of the things that you were trying to get done need to get done; could you come over and see me and talk about how we might put some actions in place that will achieve this?" He reinitiated the relationship and we had a 30-second let-bygones-be-bygones. It didn't last any longer that that. And away we went back to work.

If I had been him, knowing what he knew and under the pressures he was under, I might have fired me, too. I mean I'm not sure where what my call would have been. But I've never had a guy so pissed at me.

ANONYMOUS A

Never, Ever Make Up Nicknames for Your Clients

One of the cardinal rules of consulting is to never, ever make up nicknames for your clients. Nicknames often come out in the worst possible ways.

Years ago when I was new to consulting, CMP assigned me to a compensation study for the State of Illinois in Springfield, the state capital. At that time, Illinois had been under the control of the Democratic Party for years and years. Also, Illinois was still a patronage state where the workers got their jobs by paying off the party hacks and pols.

Our offices were in the Secretary of State's office building. He was the male version of the old maid. He lived by himself in one of the local hotels, never had a house. Well, while we were on the project, he died. Lo and behold, when going through his possessions they found millions of dollars stuffed in shoe boxes in the closet of his hotel room. He was forever known after that as Shoe Box Powell. He is a legend in Illinois politics. But I digress.

Richard Ogilvie was elected as the first Republican governor in years in 1968. He saw it as his mandate to clean up the state. This included eliminating patronage and the compensation job we were doing was a key part of this effort. Ogilvie brought in a new team, mostly young, enthusiastic and idealistic, to help him. One of these young men was assigned to coordinate our project. As time went on, he began to wear a bit thin, and the consulting team began to refer to him as Numb Nuts. "You'll never guess what Numb Nuts did today. What did Numb Nuts want this time?" And so on.

The client's building had automatic elevators and a patronage worker who pushed the buttons for us as we went from floor to floor manned each elevator car. The guy working our elevator bank was named Frank. He was in his 70s, and was on crutches. He no doubt needed a paycheck, but it wasn't really a job. To complete the background for this story, our partner-in-charge was a former Marine, husky, and he had a very short temper.

One night we were all working late including the full team, the client coordinator (Numb Nuts), and our partner. About nine o'clock we decided to quit and left as a group in the same elevator. One of the younger guys asked where Frank was? Another said he was off in the evenings. The younger consultant talking without thinking said, "Looks like the only way to get a job with the state is to stand around and look useless." Then realizing what he said and trying to cover, he turned around to Numb Nuts and blurted out, "Oh no, Numb Nuts, I didn't mean you."

Needless to say, it seemed like forever before that elevator reached the ground floor and the client coordinator, taken aback, went on his way. But, it seemed even longer as our partner ripped each and every one of us from one end to the other. I thought we were all going to be fired.

So the rule is, always refer to your clients in the most glowing of terms. Wonderful. Brilliant. Thoughtful. Honest. Strong. That way if you make a mistake, it's a good one.

By the way, this client coordinator made a career in state government. Years later, he along with several others, was indicted for alleged fraud in the Motor Vehicles Department. It seems that driver's licenses were being sold to non-qualified commercial drivers for cash bribes. You know, we were right on when we named him Numb Nuts.

RICHARD METZLER

-5-

Presentations, Meetings, and Moments Not to Be Forgotten

"Any presentation is a final exam."

ROBERT ARNOLD

From cold calls to sales presentations, from progress reports to final recommendations, consultants are geared to the big show, the moment when they step on stage and demonstrate to everyone what they can do. It is one of the highs of the business. Accordingly, this chapter explores the critical place presentations have in the consultant's repertoire.

Our contributors share some of what they've learned about the myriad, often unexpected challenges that can arise in the course of presentations and meetings. Of course, in consulting there is a lot of the unexpected.

Consultants use presentations to motivate their clients, to simplify complicated issues or bring information together in new ways. But often more "streetwise" people skills enter into play, as consultants negotiate their way through thickets of internal politics, personalities, and situations where survival means thinking on your feet. It's all about the art of communication.

If you work as a consultant long enough, you're also going to have your share of unforgettable moments, experiences with clients etched for better or for worse in memory. Everything from being told your work is the best the client has ever seen, to the more infamous miscalculations, mistakes, and mishaps inevitable even over the course of the most successful careers. What's it like to be young and so full of ideas that you spend a half hour talking over the heads of a group of police executives? How do you handle a former admiral schooled in the methods of deep intimidation? Our contributors share what they've learned from such encounters.

Consultants also face other challenges, such as when they are used as bearers of bad news, scapegoats for cost cutting agendas, for example, or to be the go-between in other tough situations. How critical is it to have the right team in place during a major presentation? What is its like to make your first sale? The best sales personalities represent a dynamic combination of ego and empathy, bringing strong self-confidence to their work, but also sensitivity to who the client is as an individual or leader.

As one veteran contributor concludes, "I learned early on to get the facts right, get them documented, and feed them back to the client very quickly." It's called earning credibility. In this chapter, we learn a few things about that.

THE PRESSURE AND THE THRILLS

Consider Any Presentation a Final Exam

I had an experience early in my career with a client that was just awful. At the time it was really devastating. We felt fortunate that they even paid the bills. In fact, during the final presentation they nearly threw us out because they didn't agree with some of the numbers we showed them. They challenged the source.

Well, the source happened to be some industry-wide data. Unfortunately, I was the guy on the spot and I hadn't anticipated they would challenge it, so I couldn't quote exact sources. And the whole thing just blew up at that point. I learned a big lesson. That is: when you go into any sort of presentation, whether it is minor or major, consider it a final exam. You have to anticipate every single question, every challenge you can think of. Early in my career I used to resent partners challenging me before going into a presentation. But after that experience, I came to look forward to it. I realized if I could get my presentation past a partner, I'm just that much better off. But what a painful lesson that was. I thought my career was over.

ROBERT ARNOLD

A Huge Rush

There are always crises to diffuse. You have to try to keep the lid on emotion and make sure people are going down the same track. I think that's the role of the senior person during a meeting or presentation, to really be alert. Of course, you want to appear to be somewhat casual and give everybody a long leash. But you also want to stay right on top of whether or not the meeting is moving toward its goals. You can let people wander for a while, but then you have to pull them back.

There's no question there is a huge rush to having a great meeting, to get your point of view across and be received well by the other side. That's great! There's a real sense of fulfillment in seeing a company have great results based on your recommendations. No question. Isn't that what keeps us doing this?

ANONYMOUS B

The Kick of the Business

Presentations were always kind of the kick of this business. There's nothing quite like sitting in front of a group of top executives trying to sell an idea.

And that is what you're doing. I mean, you're not there selling farm machinery. You're selling concepts and ideas, and usually these are very, very bright and demanding people, and you're on the hot seat. To me, that was just an incredibly exciting situation to be in. You have to be mentally adept enough to deal with their challenges.

The crowds can be tough, too. You're out pitching some proposal, a new sale opportunity or an idea or recommendation to a client that might cost them $100 million to implement, naturally, that can be pretty tough. There were some meetings that you look back on and think, that wasn't a lot of fun.

Clients also have unique cultures. Say you get into the investment banking world or the trading area of financial institutions. They have a relatively low tolerance for things that they don't see as having an immediate impact. They are out there making trades that can produce $100 million worth of revenue and $20 million worth of profit.

Speaking of a tough crowd, our firm gets involved with community organizations. It's part of making a contribution outside of business. On one occasion a number of years ago, we were working with a local group in a poor urban community. The organization was doing just wonderful things to help people develop job skills and get educated and pull themselves up by their own bootstraps.

Well, I had been invited to attend a board meeting to meet with this organization. But what nobody told me at the time was that most of the members of the board were leaders of the major gangs in this community. So I showed up for a board meeting and, let me tell you, that was an uncomfortable couple of hours. These were folks that normally you would not want to fool around with. In a sense, they were part of the leadership infrastructure of that community, and ostensibly they were there to help the community. So that's the way it was. But that was probably the toughest group that I ever had to present to. You had to wonder if you were going to get out of there alive.

DAVID TIERNO

You Have to Think On the Fly

In almost all client situations, you have to think on the fly. At our firm, we deal with CEOs and they're always asking questions you don't anticipate. There is just no way you can anticipate all the questions. The key is to have in place the right team with the right experience. Of course, you can anticipate the questions from the junior people. Sometimes you can just blow them off, too. But when you get to the senior levels they're going to ask you questions and you have to answer them. You have to have strong people with good experience and you have to trust that you're going to be able to come up with answers. And if you can't, then you've got to say you can't.

There's always an edge when you're in the middle of being grilled. There are times when you have great confidence in your team and your own knowledge. And then there are times when you don't. The worst feeling is to be in a meeting with senior people when you don't have confidence in the people around you. That can be horrifying. You just sit and worry. You try not to do that very often, but it is going to happen now and then. I know when we started, our reach often exceeded our grasp. We took some chances on pitching work, and we didn't always have the right horses. We also didn't know each other particularly well. So we would live a bit in fear. I think all of that has changed now. I'm very comfortable now.

ANONYMOUS B

They Really Love Me

Making a presentation or a proposal is like being in the feeling of the hunt. It's that great desire to go in there and compete and persuade. It's like Sally Fields at the Oscars proclaiming, "They love me, they really love me!" You want that feeling of approval. You want the client to really embrace your ideas and want to work with you. Someone I know once described a good salesperson as a person with a huge ego who is also a very sensitive person with a lot of empathy. In your work, you rely on that empathetic ability to get inside a person's shoes, to see what they're going to respond to. And then you conduct yourself accordingly.

If you think about it, that's what it takes to be a good salesperson. It is also what you're doing in consulting, selling your ideas. Selling business. Of course, I'm sure you've met plenty of people who have a big ego and are just abrasive as hell. You wouldn't want to work with them in a million years, even if they could help you. You do have to have a big ego but you also have to be empathetic.

You also should be energized by the fact that you're doing what you do because it's the right course. You want to make your clients the heroes, as opposed to just having yourself standing up declaring, "Hey, if it wasn't for me you guys wouldn't be doing this." Start doing that and your business life is going to be rather limited.

PETER SCOTT

What the _____ Are You Doing Here?

Not many people remember that the Davis-Besse Nuclear Station outside Toledo, Ohio, had a very serious incident years ago. Three Mile Island got all of the notoriety, but Davis-Besse was perilously close behind.

Typically, in those days, when a nuclear station got into trouble, the utility had to go through a work-out program with the Nuclear Regulatory Commission. They would bring in a retired admiral from the Navy, loads of engineers and operations people, and spend tremendous amounts of money to get issues fixed. There seemed to be a direct correlation between how much money was spent and how well the NRC viewed the station and its management team.

In the aftermath of this spending orgy, the utility would have to file a rate case with the state public utility commission to recover these dollars with cost-of-service adjustments. Our firm built up a substantial practice serving the utilities as regulatory strategists and witnesses. We would help build the case for complete recovery of costs and work with the lawyers and regulatory staff to put on the case before the state regulators.

Admiral Hyman Rickover created the nuclear Navy. He was a brilliant man, of course. But his main claim to fame was the tremendous intimidation to which he would subject all his officers. All officer candidates for the nuclear Navy would have to go meet the admiral before they were chosen and most went back a number of times as they rose through the ranks. He even had the front legs of the chairs in front of his desk cut off so that whoever was going through the drill would have a tendency to slip off onto the floor. This practice of intimidation carried over to all of those who worked with him over the years including the admiral brought in to clean up Davis-Besse.

Our firm and team were picked by Toledo Edison management and their outside attorneys to work with them during the rate case. But, before final selection, we had to go meet with the admiral a la Rickover. I was the partner in charge, so I got the call.

I showed up for the meeting 15 minutes early and was told to cool my heels for at least 30 or 45 minutes. I was then escorted into his office whereupon he continued working of his desk for at least 15 more minutes. He never looked up or acknowledged my presence. Finally, he raised his eyes and stared at me for at least another minute or two. Just looked. And then at the top of his lungs, he yelled, "What the _____ are you doing here?"

Fortunately, I had worked with other admirals in the past and had been warned about this admiral in particular. I stared back for 15 to 30 seconds and replied, "I head a team of regulatory experts and we're here to save your sorry ____."

The admiral glared another minute or two (it seemed longer) and finally said, "Good, when do we start?"

I replied, "I started billing you the minute I walked into your office."

Finally he grinned and we got along just fine for the duration of the project. But if I had even so much as blinked, I would have been sent packing.

RICHARD METZLER

"Thank you, Bentley. We get the picture."

Nobody Else In the Room

I once signed a contract to develop a strategy for an outsourcing consultant. It was just an unbelievable negotiation process. Really drilling down into what we were going to do. The first step was to go in and interview ten of their senior managers. These guys ran huge data centers servicing a number of different clients. They were obviously very busy.

Well, I'm all prepared for my first meeting, with all my charts and questions; all kinds of good stuff. I'm ready to kick it off. The first guy walks in and tells me he wants to make one thing clear before we begin. First, he doesn't think they need me, they can do this stuff themselves. But since I'm here, he just wants me to know that if I'm going to waste his time, he's out of here. So that's how we began.

The line or comeback I used on him was just to thank him for being so frank. I told him I really appreciated his openness. I told him I had put together a set of questions and some tools that I thought were useful, and hoped he would find them useful, too. With that, I said, if you're ready, we can get started. Basically, I just tried to diffuse the situation. And it worked. The guy just sat down and said, okay I'm ready, let's go.

I should add that I didn't have backup on that engagement, either. I was the lead consultant. There was an engagement manager from the client side. We usually insisted on having an engagement manager at our firm, as well as on the client's side. But in this case there was nobody else in the room except the two of us: me, and the man I was interviewing.

As it turned out, we ended up taking the allotted time. He even insisted on setting up a follow-up meeting. So, despite how it began, it worked out very well. When I walked into this assignment, however, I thought, what did I get myself into here! And the rest of the guys were just as cantankerous. It was a very demanding situation.

MICHAEL ALBRECHT

I Haven't Tanked a Company Yet

I have done a certain amount of work for companies in serious trouble, where they believed that if they could just move away from all this, so to speak, their problems would evaporate. It's like the married couple having troubles that decides, well, if we just move to Denver, all our problems will go away and we can start over. Of course, they go to Denver and find they've brought all their problems with them.

There's a corporate version of that, which says, if we could just move away from all this crap and refocus on the things that are important to business, we'll succeed. One of the companies that came to us years ago was American Motors, at the time the fourth-largest automobile manufacturer in the United States. The fourth horse in a three-horse race, actually. Back then the U.S. auto market was just being eaten alive by the Japanese, so whenever any newspaper article had to be written on how badly the industry was going, they would cite American Motors, and show pictures of an American Motors plant. The company was an easy target. Renault owned half of the company and they were backing off because it was a disaster for them. They'd put in a new board, which included their own people and an American CEO who'd come out of the company's marketing arm. He was very bright and capable, but extremely volatile.

He believed part of the problem was they were being too identified with the American automobile industry, when they were really producing French cars in America. Thus, if they could only be seen as a French company, he reasoned - an import company-they would do better. So, what better way to attain that image than to move away from Detroit? He had the idea of moving the company to Louisville.

It was in this context that we were brought in by one of the top people there, to kind of bell the cat, and point out to this CEO that his plan was basically nuts. Nobody had said that, but it was apparent. So we went ahead and did our analysis, and we were to come in and give our presentation. But something had transpired between the time we were told of the meeting and when it actually happened, because everybody was there. About 30 or 40 people. A lot of people we hadn't seen before.

I stood up in my opening comments and said, "We've been hired to help you decide whether it's wise to move American Motors from Detroit or not. Of course, to move this company, one of three things has to happen for it to make sense: 1) You have to be able to sell more cars; 2) you have to be able to sell cars for more money; or 3) you have to be able to manufacture cars for less." At which point this guy who I'd never seen before stood up in the room, looked at me and said, very sharply, "What is this, a joke?" He then turned on his heels and walked out.

I didn't know who this guy was or what he was talking about. I found out later he was a former controller. Actually, we did show that the theories of the CEO were probably correct. They could feasibly sell more cars if they moved. But the risks involved in moving were very high. The risk of not being able to put new cars into production—which their future depended on— or at least at a lower cost, was very high. It was such a threat that moving was not a wise thing to do. We had to deftly show the CEO that his argument was right, but that there were also other considerations.

When we finished our presentation, he said, "Well, we need to look more at the implications of moving before we make this decision." He was able to back down gracefully and then let the issue die. It was one of those cases where you're proud because you've done something very difficult. In this case, going toe-to-toe against the CEO in public, and then giving him a way out. It was a big success. Especially considering the bizarre comment early on from someone who looked fairly senior.

These are the types of situations you encounter. But I guess I've done okay. I haven't tanked a company yet.

FORD HARDING

STORIES OF GREAT PRESENTATIONS

At A Loss for Words

Eddie Carlson, the President and CEO of United Airlines, was as beloved by his people as any CEO I've ever worked with. He had a capability of making everybody love him and to want to do their absolute best for him. Our consulting team felt the same way.

He was elected President shortly after the Airline Deregulation Act of 1974. Prior to that, airlines functioned as a cost of service business, allowed to earn a return of their capital subject to regulatory rules and regulations. Because they were allowed to charge for all expenses and because they were assured a return on their investments, the airlines really didn't know or care who their customers were or where their revenues came from. Conditions obviously changed radically after the industry was deregulated.

Just getting to the presentation was an ordeal. We worked all weekend to get ready for the Monday morning presentation. We experienced all the normal problems—partners disagreeing, copying machines breaking down, etc. So finally we finished early Monday morning and ran out the door to catch a taxi from downtown Chicago out to United's headquarters in Elk Grove. We were beating on this poor driver to speed it up, cut through lanes, and lay on the horn. We even promised an extra $10. Well, we made it, but the only reason we were on time was that the clocks changed on Saturday night and we gained an hour.

Our project was to analyze their markets, customers, travel agents, and sources of revenues. The basic approach was to use a flow chart that tracked all entities and volumes from start to finish. This intrigued everybody at United including Eddie Carlson. We spent far more time than the 60 minutes that he would normally devote to any subject. He was at the front of the room looking at the projected slide on the screen and asking questions of everybody in the room. From a consultant's point of view, it was one those very rare situations where you and the client were totally involved and in sync. It was just wonderful.

Finally, after many hours, Eddie turned around to my partner in charge, Nick Radell, and said, "I've worked with a lot of consultants over the years but this is the best piece of work I've ever seen."

I stood there dumbfounded for the longest time, and finally replied, "Mr. Carlson, I came prepared for everything but a compliment."

Laughing, everybody in the room agreed that it was the first time that they had ever seen me at a loss for words.

RICHARD METZLER

The Hunt Is Better Than the Kill

To sum up, I think the hunt is much better than the kill. I mean, the selling part is just really fun.

One time we were making a presentation for a proposal to a city council. The whole job had really come out of nowhere, and our guy gave a crappy proposal. But we still got the job.

The city council grilled us on all kinds of questions, like where are you staying and how much does it cost a night. And then at the end, we were awarded $1.2 million. And we said, we need $2 million. So then the city manager asked us in a private meeting, well, how much do you really need? We said, well, we really need $2.2 million. He says, okay, we can work that out. So he just gave us another million dollars in what was basically a 30-second conversation. That was great.

I suppose if we had asked for $3 million, we probably would have gotten it.

JAMES BLOMBERG

Like a Wedding Reception

Once I was trying to sell some work to a large equipment defense supplier, which was seeking to relocate to reduce costs, particularly labor costs. They were under contract with Local Five of the UAW, and we had been trying to do business with them for some time. Locals are numbered from the date of origin, so this was the fifth oldest UAW local in the nation.

I'd been there several times meeting with different levels of management. But every time I thought it was sold, I would have to meet with someone else, all of which was prior to a final meeting with the CEO.

Apparently, they were afraid to put anyone in front of the CEO. He had them all terrorized. Finally, I was told to come in for one last presentation at which he would be present. It was a circumstance where my flight had arrived late the night before, and I didn't get to sleep until three in the morning. I then had a three-hour drive to their facility the next morning, which meant I had to leave at the crack of dawn. On top of that, I was down with the flu.

When I arrived for the meeting, the CEO was sitting at the table with all his underlings on either side of him, all lined up. They're all watching him like hawks. It was obvious their only concern was his reaction to things. Well, I got about a third of the way into my presentation when the CEO suddenly looked up and said, "I don't know why we're wasting our time with this. Why don't we just buy the XYZ building (which was about 50 miles down the road) and be done with all this?"

Now, this was an insane idea. If their cost strategy was to succeed, they had to get away from the union. And there was just no way they could do that with such a move. Now I was on the spot. Finally, I said to myself, screw it. I'm tired, I'm sick, I've been through six meetings to get to this guy and now it's all going down the tank. I had to respond. In a very calm voice, I said, "Frankly, I think it would be very naive to think you could do what you need to do at that location." Well, there was dead silence in the room. Everybody just looked up at the ceiling or down at their papers.

The CEO just stared at me. He didn't say anything. So, I just went on with my presentation. Another five minutes went by. Suddenly, he just stood up and announced that he thought we should get started on this project right away. Then he walked out of the room. The meeting was over. Well, everybody starting coming up to me then, shaking my hand, saying what a great presentation. It was like a wedding reception!

Of course, none of this had anything to do with the presentation. It had to do with that question. The question was a test. The CEO was testing my backbone. He wanted to see whether I would stand up to him and give him honest advice. If I had waffled for a second, we would have been dead.

This is something you see in this profession. The client will find a way to put you to the test. You know, when you buy a car, you can go out and test drive it. When you buy a computer you can go down to the store, tinker with it, check it out. But when you buy a consulting service, you don't really know what it's going to be like until after you've bought it. So the individual consultants become a kind of proxy for the service, a way to test the firm's mettle, so to speak. The test always comes as kind of a surprise and it might involve any number of things, except it is always about you. It is not about your firm or your methodology or anything. It is about you personally.

FORD HARDING

Can You Start Tomorrow?

We had one client for whom we had done some analysis, and we had been called back. It was a privately owned company. We had the three owners sitting there and we made our pitch. As it turned out, it was obviously a bigger project than they had anticipated. They said they had to talk about it and asked us to wait in the conference room. When the client is hesitating like this, the ploy I have used a few times is to say something like how we can usually plan and begin a project in about as much time as it will take them just to make the decision that they want to do it. Try to reassure them. So we waited and they talked. Finally, they came back. The three of them looked at each other, then one of them spoke, "Okay, we want to do it. Can you start tomorrow?" This was, I believe, a Thursday. Now I was really sweating! I said, "Well, actually, would Monday be all right?" We had gone from hesitation to jumping into the fire, just like that.

COBY FRAMPTON

His Mind Was Faster Than Ours

When the client is the problem – that's the toughest job in consulting. I've faced that a couple of times in my career and it's very difficult. At times you can Arabesque around the client to get to a more senior level. Or you can convince the client to take personal counseling. At times it's just an unsolvable problem. There are times when if that person is so entrenched in both their ideas and position, you can't change it.

I vividly remember a piece of work we did for a large homebuilder. We were brought in because data processing was out of control. The company was run by a fellow who had started out as a carpenter and had built the business up over the years. A brilliant, self-made man. But what we discovered was that the problem was actually him. He was continually undermining the data processing people. He would come in and pull the paperwork in the middle of a print run, pull it right out of the printer, and just leave things in a mess. There was no way they could run an efficient shop.

We also learned there was a high turnover because the owner showed little respect for his employees. We struggled with this and after about three weeks finally met with the audit partner. This fellow was a cigar smoker and he nearly swallowed his cigar when we told him the problem was the company president. He said, "I called you in for four weeks to help on data processing, and you're telling me to fire the president of my biggest client."

After a lot of convincing, we finally scheduled a breakfast meeting at the president's house. His wife served us breakfast and we sat out on his porch. Then he asked us, "Okay, what's wrong with data processing?" I had to look at him and say, well, actually, it's you. That was tough. But he listened, and we ended up talking the whole day. Finally, that same day, he came to me and said, "You know, you're right. The problem isn't just data processing. I may be a great homebuilder, but I'm a lousy manager. I want to think about this and then I'm going to act on what I've learned."

Two weeks later he resigned as president of the company. He made himself chairman and got involved in starting a new division in multi-housing, which didn't involve managing a lot of people. And he went out and became one of the largest builders of multi-family housing around. A bigger company ultimately acquired the firm.

But thank God he had the courage to face the situation and act on it. I had anticipated we'd have to work through the problem with him, but his mind was faster than ours. He was truly brilliant, a man who had built a company with his own hands. Another client might have thrown us out.

"Would you mind stepping outside while we tear your proposal to shreds?"

We actually never came to the point of recommending that he resign. I don't know what we really recommended. But he beat us to it. Ideally, recommendations should be no surprise. For that reason, I think it's important to stay in frequent contact with your client. The happiest presentation is one in which the client already knows the answer and it's really a stage act where everybody is playing out roles but the answer has been well established.

EDWARD PRINGLE

That First Sale

A high point would be when I moved from just being a consultant assigned to a project to the person who sold the assignment. To get to that point where I could finally say, I've brought home some work. You get a real rush the first time you do that. I recall on this occasion that we had done quite a bit of analysis for our proposal. And our presentation was done before a large group, maybe about 12 to 15 people from the client organization.

When we finished the presentation, which took about an hour, they asked us if we wouldn't mind stepping out of the room while they talked it over. I think everybody on our team thought, okay, they're going to let us down easy. I remember I had been looking around the room during the presentation, trying to read what was happening, trying to read the body language, the facial expressions. But it was all just a wash. Half the people looked like they agreed, half looked like they didn't. You just couldn't tell.

I felt almost like you do when you're waiting for your first child to be born; actually, worse than having your first child. At least in that situation somebody else is doing most of the work.

Well, when they brought us back in, they all had smiles on their faces. Only then did I really know we had done it. They'd been so poker faced about it. They said we're going to go ahead with your project now. I recall the first thing I wanted to do was get to a telephone and call my wife. What a great moment!

In those early days, making a presentation like that, you've got the giddies, anticipating and hoping everything goes right. You're saying to yourself, is there anything else that I might have done? Could I have prepared better somehow? Did I address or focus on the right person in the room? Over time I think I've learned to be more interactive, to back up a bit if I have to. You know, if I see someone who looks they're not sure they agree with what I'm saying, I'll stop right there and clear up whatever's on their mind.

But that first sale was a gutwrencher.

COBY FRAMPTON

STORIES OF NOT-SO-GREAT PRESENTATIONS

It Was Just a Bloodbath

There was another situation with a manufacturing client who was very proud of the fact that they had the lowest IT expenditures to revenue of almost anyone in the industry. But they wanted to tighten that even more. They thought they were getting better value than any of their competitors, but actually they were not. What they were doing was driving IT into the ground. And it was our challenge to demonstrate that to them.

When we met with the senior management team, all these grizzled, old manufacturing guys, their attitude was you'd better demonstrate. You better have the data. In our presentation, the question we posed up front was: Are you getting better value than your competitors out of your IT investment? I asked the question and then I put a big NO on the screen.

From there we got into the data, demonstrating that it was a pipe dream. If they wanted to get their organization into a manageable position, they had better start to invest more in IT. Of course, we knew by then what their record was in the user community. We knew the failures they had in trying to implement IT and why. We were armed. And that is what you have to be. You have to know exactly why you're making a recommendation. It's just too easy to walk into a situation, make a quick assessment, and come back with a recommendation. There's a tendency for some people to go in and do that. They listen to one individual and then say, all right, here's what you should do.

We had one engagement where we got smacked across the forehead because we made our recommendations before we fully understood the data. The problem was our client had been a former consultant. He called us in because he just didn't have the time to uncover and analyze all the data and come to some decent conclusion. So he called us in because he knew us. But we were kind of shooting from the hip. By the time I got involved in it, it was just a blood bath. I mean, the guy just wanted to kill our consultant. I went into the situation trying to figure out a way to recover.

MICHAEL ALBRECHT

He Began Crying

I can share one story on scripting and role-playing that comes to mind. Years ago the chairman and I were working with the executive committee of the board of directors of a closely-held company. That is, it was a third generation company with lots of family members. Years before, they had hired a professional manager as chairman who, by this time, was in his late seventies. He'd suffered a debilitating stroke several years before and it was just time for him to go. The problem was the executive committee didn't have the guts to fire him.

So basically they hired us to get rid of the chairman. That was the hidden agenda. We had it all wrapped up with the gloss of a strategic plan, an organizational study and other things. But the core recommendation was that it was time for this fellow to go. Part of the challenge was, how are we going to play this out? We knew this man was extremely emotional, and we really had to plan our response. You know, which way were we going to dive if he pulled out a pistol and started shooting.

Honestly, we were very concerned about his response. Well, do you know what he did? He cried. He just teared up and began crying. That was almost more difficult to deal with than had he pulled out a gun. Or if he'd just gotten angry, which we had fully expected.

Well, we didn't apologize for the recommendation. We just tried to offer some remarks to soften the blow. You know, how difficult we knew this to be. How in all of our careers and in all of our lives there comes a time when changes must take place. I knew I was in charge of the situation but I also knew I had to be compassionate. But for this to come from a 28-year old to a person in his 70s was probably a bitter pill. Ultimately, in a situation like that, there's only so much softening you can do.

JERRY JACKSON

Escort Me Out of Town

Quite early in my consulting career, the partner who was in charge of my group called me in with what he portrayed as an excellent opportunity. A local school district, perhaps 100 miles from Chicago, wanted to hire an outside consultant to do a study of their buildings and grounds. It was described to me as a chance to show the firm that I was ready to be more independent and that I could close a sale on my own. The other partners were all "too busy" to help out.

So off I went, and I sold the project. It was my very first sale on my own. I was rather proud of myself. But it turned out that it really was a janitorial and lawn maintenance study. The new school superintendent, hired from outside of the town, thought the school was dirty and poorly maintained, and he was correct. One of the main problems was that the staff worked only on the day shift when all the classrooms were occupied. By the time the classrooms emptied out, the staff was out of the building as well. The only way to get the cleaning needed was to pay overtime and hold the janitors over. That, of course, was killing the school's budget. The changes that were needed were obvious. But the local union was dead set against any changes. People's lives would be disrupted if they had to work the afternoon shift.

We eventually came to the big presentation to the school board. I think everybody in town was there, including the local newspaper and radio station. The meeting was contentious. Fists were being shaken, curses were being thrown, all mostly at me. And I'm thinking to myself, this is another fine fix to be in. No kidding, I was scared. And after the meeting I would have to go out to the parking lot, get in my car, and drive home.

The superintendent then tells me that he will call the police, and they will escort me safely out of town. I meet the officer at the door and he tells me that he will get me to the city limits after which I'm on my own. He also tells me that his sister is married to one of the janitors and she is definitely not happy with her husband working afternoons.

I ask him to get me as far as the down ramp onto the expressway, and say I'll make it from there. I have never driven a car as fast as that night, either before or since, 100 miles per hour back toward Chicago. And no, I definitely did not go back for follow-up business.

RICHARD METZLER

Say What?

After I was in the business for maybe four to six months I really thought I was hot stuff. So I did a presentation for a team of police executives in Baton Rouge, Louisiana. My speech today is probably toned down compared to the speed it was back then. But I was 22 years old at the time and just loaded with data and I wanted to get it all out. It was my first real opportunity to be in the limelight, and I wanted to give all of my perspectives. So I went on for about a half hour. I also never really looked at my audience. They teach you to look at your audience and adapt to them, but I didn't. I just had to get my presentation out. I had slides and all sorts of stuff.

At the end of the half hour, I went through my concluding comments and then asked if there were any questions. The police chief looked up, speaking for the group, and the first words out of his mouth were, "Say what?"

I had gone on and on and these guys had heard nothing and understood nothing. That was a good lesson for me. You have to learn to adapt, to play to your audience, and understand their culture. Fortunately, I learned it early in my career.

LANNY COHEN

He Had To Catch a Plane

One of my very first client meetings was actually quite memorable. The president of the client company had made a presentation describing how the company was doing. The partner in charge of the consulting project then stood up and lambasted this client, saying how stupid they were, and listing all the mistakes they were making. He really put this guy down.

After this broadside, the partner then announced he had to run off to catch his plane. So he just left us there to clean up the damage. He set up this horrible dynamic and then dumped it in our laps. He was a brilliant guy but he came from academia and I think lacked a certain common sense.

I think how you say what you have to say is as important as what you have to say. I learned a lot of important lessons from that experience. Our work is always a partnership. It can never be an "us" versus "them" situation, or about how much smarter we are than you. If you don't get to a true relationship of trust with your client, then you're not going to be very helpful or successful. You have to work with your client.

WAYNE COOPER

The Vice President Was Fired

I remember one situation with a client on Wall Street in which we were doing an operations review. As part of the review we did an analysis of expenses and found some inappropriate expenditures. They were actually way out of line. This was a securities business so we knew there was going to be a lot of sensitivity about the issue, in terms of stocks.

We met with the CEO and the vice president of operations at the CEO's request. It was at the end of the day on a Friday at their headquarters. The vice president was basically responsible for all of these expenditures. And the CEO fired the vice president, right in front of our eyes! The

CEO had security escort this guy to his office, clean it out, and then he was escorted right out of the building.

I got a little nervous because it was rumored that this guy was connected to the mob. You know, we didn't want to start our cars for a while. We joked about it but it was actually quite serious. After all, we were the reason this guy was fired, so there was reason for concern.

Of course, the CEO didn't have to have us sitting there at that meeting. But we were his proof in the pudding and he wanted us there. All of us on that project were very nervous for a while. But, as you can see, I'm still here. So I guess it turned out for the best.

WILLARD ARCHIE

We Never Got the Work

When I think back, I wonder sometimes how I survived some of the experiences. I remember giving a sales presentation to a non-profit hospital system here in Chicago. I was standing up there going through the proposal, detailing our objectives and the scope and approach we would take. Well, one of the people in the back of the room asked how long all this would take. But the question wasn't clear and I thought he asked how much this will take, meaning in terms of price.

I started into a discussion about how we had worked all this out, the plan of approach and the timetable. I think we were making a good impression. But because I had misunderstood the question, I then went on and told him what the price would be. Well, the client didn't want everyone in the room to know that. We never got the work.

Unfortunately, there are as many of those famous moments in consulting as there are good ones.

ROBERT ARNOLD

Stories That Are Unusual

Served With a Subpoena

We all have won projects that we shouldn't have and we all have lost projects that we shouldn't have. But over the years it all adds up. If you're good at what you do, you get more than your fair share. But here's a story about a very unusual way to lose a sale. I guarantee you that this has never happened to anyone else.

We had developed a field and customer services program, the key part of which was a new and sophisticated mapping system. We could overlay a client's service territory and facilities, the local transportation and road system, and most important of all the customers and their required service levels. I conceived of this product when I saw the mapping system company give a demonstration for a totally different application. I assigned our engineers and software folks to execute the program and it was a huge sales success. We would turn it on and show the potential client what we could do. All of the utilities engineers loved it.

We had set up a demonstration for this one particular client. All of the top management team attended from the CEO down several layers. In a word, the presentation was "fantastic." They were completely involved. Questions flew nonstop. They suggested new uses that hadn't occurred to us. It was great. And we were moving to the closing of the sale stage. Words like who would be on the team, where we would set up the project office, and how much this would cost. Old hands at the consulting business can generally smell the sale, and this was in the bag. I was counting the dollars.

Then the CEO's secretary came into the conference room and gave the boss a folded over message. He opened it and his face turned white. He packed up his papers and left the room without even saying goodbye. Well, of course, the meeting dragged from there. Nobody was going to make a decision without the CEO being there and blessing it. We left muttering to ourselves and asking what the hell happened.

As it happened, we stayed overnight in the town. The next morning we went down for breakfast and when we opened the local newspaper, there was the CEO's picture on the front page. The story was that he had been served a subpoena by the local courts for alleged sexual harassment of his former personal assistant. If the law had been 20 minutes later in showing up we would have closed the sale.

RICHARD METZLER

DILBERT: © Scott Adams/Dist. By United Feature Syndicate, Inc.

That Bomb Scare Was the Best Thing

I remember one time we went out for a mid-project review of what we were doing for a telecom group. The client contact was the chief operating officer. He thought it was a final report because his assistant didn't have the nerve to tell him that it was just a mid-point review, not the final report. So we're going through this discussion on the top floor of this 30-story building. We're sitting there and this guy is just ripping into our work, saying, this is terrible, this sucks. We're trying to tell him that this is just the mid-point review, but this guy doesn't listen well. All of sudden, his secretary comes in and says, you ought to know that we just got a call. There's a bomb scare and they're evacuating the building. So we ran down 30 flights of stairs and had a beer across the way and then went home. Considering how things were going that bomb scare was probably the best thing that could have happened to us.

JAMES BLOMBERG

Working With Ray—His Story

I was involved in a study of the purchasing department at the Tennessee Valley Authority (TVA). I was the account manager, Dick Metzler was the project leader, and there was another fellow named Len Wass. Actually, I had a lot of different jobs going on then, so Dick and Len really did the project by themselves. I just interviewed a few people. After Dick and Len did all their fact-finding analysis, the three of us put the report together. Basically, they briefed me as I was going to do the presentation to the head of purchasing, let's call him Rex. He was a big guy and a former army officer.

On the day of the presentation, Rex called together all of his staff. It was a very large purchasing department—perhaps 100 or 120 people. A number of our recommendations right at the outset were organizational recommendations. Normally, the TVA people stood in their jobs forever. It was a quasi-governmental organization, and hence the people didn't rotate to new jobs or new positions. Once you became a manager you stayed a manager, more or less for life.

In spite of this culture, we had recommended a lot of changes. So Rex had convened his whole staff. He sat to the side while I was up at this podium reporting on our findings. Dick and Len were sitting right next to me. While I was talking and explaining what we recommended, I was watching Rex. I could just tell that he wasn't going to do anything. He was going to read this report, put it on the shelf, and not really do anything we recommended, especially the organizational changes. I knew he just felt he was obligated to do a study, but wasn't particularly eager to make a lot of changes. He liked the way things were, I guess. He was probably just pleasing a boss of his who had asked for the study. You could say it was a typical governmental situation.

So, when I got to the end, he asked if there was anything else to say. So I said, "Well, actually, Rex, I'll tell you one thing that all the fellows here, all the people we interviewed, told us."

He asked, "What was that?"

I said, "They all said that you don't have the balls to put in these recommendations." Dick and Len were looking at one another like where the hell did I get that? The people we interviewed didn't tell me that. Even if it were true, I hadn't even interviewed enough people to know it. Obviously, I was lying, which I was.

But Rex jumped up. "I'll show you guys who has the balls!" he declared. And he did what we asked. Unfortunately, that ploy is only good once a career. It's not something you can pull too often.

RAYMOND EPICH

Working With Ray—The Prequel

As Ray mentioned, Len Wass and I did all the work on the TVA project. As the partner, Ray just came in at key times, primarily the presentations. What Ray didn't say was that Len and I made the same presentation the day before to the whole staff but without Rex.

For background, TVA was just embarking on their huge nuclear construction program. They were going to build eight new nuclear units in a matter of only ten years. Complicating matters, TVA's procurement procedures were written into the Act by the U.S. Congress in the 1930's. It required, for example, that any item valued over $25 had to be competitively bid through the mails to multiple sources. As you can imagine, the paperwork associated with this effort was tremendous. And the build up of personnel was also tremendous. We were there to find ways to simplify their procedures, to keep the staff buildup in check, and to make the system faster and more efficient. And if changes were to be made, the two Senators from Tennessee would have to sponsor legislation to the Congress.

Internally, the Purchasing Department had divided into two camps. In the first camp were the "progressives" who wanted to make the changes. The second camp was made up of the "old guard" who wanted to leave things as they were. The number two man in the Purchasing Department was an old guard member. He had joined the TVA in the 1930's when it was originally created. TVA was the only job he ever had. He viewed the TVA as an almost sacred or holy organization. Any changes would be heresy.

So, back to our presentation. As you would expect, we proposed rather wide-sweeping revisions to people, organization, and processes. All through the presentation, we were peppered by questions and comments from the old guard. And the number two man's face got redder by the minute. He was boiling. Finally, he jumped to his feet and screamed at me, "You're a g__ d___, no good Yankee m_____ f_____!" And he stormed out of the conference room.

All of our staff agreed that it was only the second time that they ever saw me speechless.

RICHARD METZLER

"Was It Anything I Said?"

There are always surprises. That's part of the excitement of the whole process. Knowing that the unknown or the unanticipated will likely happen. And then how well did you deal with it? You can do an awful lot of planning and thinking, and you need to do that. But there is just no way that you'll ever identify everything that can go wrong. You can also spend way too much time thinking about everything that can go wrong, and not enough about everything that can go right. Obviously, this is not a business for someone with a high fear of failure or embarrassment.

So yes, surprises do happen. Maybe it's just as well this one didn't involve me. A friend of mine, Bob Jacoby, was in the middle of giving a presentation to a state-wide public power board. Most of the members of this board were local Nebraskans. Farmers, actually. The average age of the board was way up there. I mean, this was a really old group of guys. Half of them were falling asleep

Apparently, Jacoby was right in the middle of his presentation when one of them passed gas in the most obnoxious way possible, just very loud. The sound just reverberated off the walls. It stopped Jacoby right in the middle of his remarks. It was almost as if he had to say something. He looked over in the direction where the sound had come from, remarking, "Was it anything in particular that I've said?" That kind of won the day with the client. It also goes to show that you have to be prepared for almost anything.

PETER SCOTT

TIPS FROM THE PROS

Consulting Is an Art Form

Tennis is a good metaphor for the give-and-take during a presentation. Tennis has an element of finality to it. You've got that plop, plop, plop, back and forth, and then it's over. Certainly there are moments of high tension when you're in effect saying, I hope this is on the money. But if you've done your homework and have confidence in your data selection and diagnosis, then you usually have faith in what you're doing.

My greater concern is usually whether we are delivering information the right way, as opposed to, is this the right information to be delivered?

Seldom am I lacking in confidence about the rightness of the information. But, I may be less certain that I've read the personality of the client correctly, so that they are getting the information the way they prefer to get information. With some people you learn that you have to say what's critical very gently, because they are fragile.

With others you have to stand up, pick up your chair, and whack them over the head with it because if you don't, they just won't get it. In between these two extremes are lots of other possibilities for what I would call the art in our work. And that's what it is. Consulting is an art form.

JERRY JACKSON

It's Bizarre

I think people should read body language books, books on dressing, and they should study group dynamics. They should cultivate listening skills and counseling skills. These are the skills of being a consultant. And they are all extremely important skills if you're going to succeed in consulting.

Eighty-five percent of what we communicate is in what we see. What we sense. When you're on the telephone you're only doing 15 percent. If you also take away the voice inflection, as with email, imagine what else you've taken away, right? You know, you can't put affect into a written message. Even where people sit in a room can matter. How the room is constructed; the geography; the sense of space in terms of the way people cooperate and behave. It's extremely important.

If you are in a meeting and you want to control someone, watch yourself if you're sitting in a circle or at a conference table. You will invariably have a fight with the person who is diagonal from you. If you know that, you can control yourself so you don't end up in a fight. It's bizarre and incredible but there is a pattern to these things.

ELIZABETH KOVACS

90 Percent of the Questions Come In the First Ten Minutes

In most cases, when you're presenting your conclusions, there are certain tactics you want to follow. One is to be aware that 90 percent of the questions come up in the first 10 minutes. So you learn to present the information or issues you are most sure of first. In any analysis, there are some things where you're on more solid ground than others. So you learn to present the issues that you have documented best first. That's usually when the questions are going to come up, when people are going to test you.

Another point is that you always want to know who is going to be there. Ideally, they're all people that you've met before. Try to introduce yourself, if you can. It's not unheard of to have a person or two show up who you weren't expecting. But you always want to find out who they are, what their interests are in the project. If you can spend a minute or two with them and get them to talk a little, it's usually very beneficial. They'll feel like they've been included more, that you're open to them. It becomes just a little more of a personal relationship.

You have to think about these things. In this business you are very often hired to deal with difficult people.

FORD HARDING

The Ground Has Shifted

All consultants dread those moments when you have to tell clients that what they are doing doesn't make sense. Who wants to be told that he or she is not very smart, particularly by some over-educated, smart-aleck consultant?

A technique I always used was to go into a fair amount of detail about the client's present strategy or program. Then I would drop back in time and lay out the set of circumstances that led them to developing and implementing this strategy or program. I would tell them that what they are now doing is exactly what they should have been doing. Then I would go on to tell them how the world has shifted over the last few years, and that they were now a little bit behind, a little bit off the mark. But now with some fine-tuning they can get right back on target.

It was amazing. As long as I told they had done well and needed only some adjustments, they would accept the recommendations. In reality, of course, the changes that were needed could be extensive. But the magic words were "fine-tuning and adjustments."

RICHARD METZLER

-6-

The Matter of Ethics

"Consultants are extremely ethical."

ALEX ZABROSKY

"It's just good business to be honest."

CARL LOBUE

"The biggest ethical issue is the interest of the client vs. the interest of the firm."

EDWARD PRINGLE

sk a veteran consultant about industry ethics and you'll get an animated, strongly voiced response: "Of course we're honest, and of course we adhere to the highest standards both personally and within our firms." It's almost an article of faith among consultants.

Ask the question a second time and you'll get a slightly different response; regardless of your own or your firm's ethical codes, being honest is simply good business. Consulting is a long-term business, and nothing is more important than the reputation of honesty. If you lose your reputation, you are out of business.

Where is this matter of ethics most important? Certain key issues come up repeatedly. As a consultant, how do you resolve what is good for the client and what is good for your consulting firm as a whole? To whom are you responsible? The client contact? The company itself? Your own firm? What if you discover the client is the problem you've been hired to "fix"? The answers aren't always obviously black and white; rather they are more nuanced. Sometimes being absolutely right now isn't the best answer for either the client or the firm in the long run.

Do you practice ethical consulting? Check out the 12 Principles of the Code of Ethics developed by and for the Association of Management Consulting Firms by Alan Andolsen, former Chairman of the Code of Ethics Committee, and other members. But first, here are some thoughts on ethics, and examples of ethical challenges that our veteran consultants faced, and how they resolved them.

CONSULTING IS AN ETHICAL BUSINESS

In the Business for the Long Haul

I believe most of those who profess to be consultants are in the business for the long haul. They're not hanging a shingle out in between other operations. I think they tend to realize that if they're not ethical, they ain't in business. But that still leaves a rather wide range for what we mean when we talk about ethics. There is a gray area in this business, instances where you have to ask questions. Is this on the borderline?

I also know there are some people who end up doing consulting who don't think about ethics much. These folks are basically in there for the money. They come in and they bomb and strafe and also don't last very long because they don't build the reputation.

In the 25 years I've been doing this, it's been my personal experience both from the business and consulting side of things that basically people are ethical. Most people may not be explicitly focused on their ethical framework per se, but when you sit down and start talking you'll find in their own way that they have an ethical structure they're working with. Of course, sometimes that is exactly what gets them into problems. But if their ethical code is to only give mgmt what it wants, and they misconstrue or misunderstand what are management's intentions, they are in trouble.

As far as working with senior management, almost universally in my experience I've been very impressed with their ethical level. I can't think of any senior executive that I ever thought wanted us to cut an ethical corner. And our client list is pretty impressive. Yes, we have been in the situation where we've had to politely disagree with clients, at the risk perhaps of losing the project. But we've never been fired from a job, so we know they're listening.

As I say, there is a kind of gray area in this business. A client might be in litigation, for example, and you find yourself in a situation where they want you to say this or that, back them up on something that's not quite right. Or, it's a matter of do you destroy records or not destroy records? And you've got to advise them no, that's not appropriate. We have to try to keep our independence in such matters. We have to stay objective.

Frankly, if you're only there to just get the fee, and are willing to say whatever they want to get that fee, you really should be questioning how you're running your firm. If you're not strong enough to stand up to a client on principles, then I think you call into question the credibility of your organization.

ALAN ANDOLSEN

Consultants Are Extremely Ethical

In my practice, I have found that consultants are extremely ethical. I do a lot of work in the confidentiality field. I've got about 100 clients, whether firms or individuals and I've seen them across the board in terms of how they operate. But without exception, consultants maintain client confidences. Everything that I've seen has always been extremely ethical.

Even when they are wrong, they're ethical. I've seen situations where consultants get involved in dispute with their clients. I have handled malpractice cases, and you know that's not the high point of a consultant's career. But I've seen those, and I've seen how consultants deal with legal situations and moral situations. When it comes down to question of integrity, they take it very seriously. For example, say a vice president or a partner of a consulting firm is accused of sexual harassment. The consulting firm doesn't care if he's the best salesperson in the world, he's out of there. They just are not going to tolerate that.

In a law firm it depends on who's sucking up to whom. And in a big corporation you might find same thing—there's always a little brownnosing. That has a very minimal play in consulting. And when these legal situations do arise, be it a malpractice case or whatever, consultants will fess up to it.

It's very difficult to restore your reputation. I mean it's almost like that Christmas party where you had one too many and had a lampshade over the head. How do you get over that? Well, it takes time.

ALEX ZABROSKY

You Build In Integrity When You Hire

We spend some time on what I won't call ethics but rather principles. We have a creed that we share with candidates, and we hope that they'll self-select out if that creed doesn't make sense to them. We go through a lot in our selection so by the time somebody comes into our organization, we feel that they're properly aligned with us. That isn't to say that our ethics are right or wrong. It's just that they're ours. Our principles are ours.

Because of how we hire, I've never had the types of problems that I've read about, where consultants milk clients. It's just not an issue. I've only had one experience with a consultant who cheated on his expense report. We don't even check expense reports anymore. We feel that if there's an issue with the client, then the consultant will deal with the client. It won't be the home office. We're hiring adults and if we do the right job of hiring, we won't have to do this kind of monitoring

What I found early on is that our typical consultant profile is generally very black and white. None of us are real good with shades of gray.

CYNTHIA DRISKILL

You Keep Your Own Score

I'm a glass is half-full kind of guy versus thinking the glass is half-empty. I think, by and large, ethics in the industry are very good. I think it's kind of like golf—it's still a "gentleman's game". You keep your own score. You call the penalties on yourself, you count the strokes.

You learn quickly if the firm you've joined has a commitment to being ethical, and if it isn't, I don't think you should stay. Give it up and move on. There've only been a couple really awful exceptions over the years, firms that were known to be bait-and-switch firms. Some time back, there were some cost-cutting firms that did work on a percentage of dollars saved basis. They'd go in and basically do job elimination work. There were only a couple of those companies within the province of consulting and they were viewed as not being very ethical about the way they worked. And there was a fair amount of bad reputation that the industry suffered due to these two companies. But those companies either went out of business or into a different line of operations.

ANONYMOUS A

We Only Build Honest Models

Several years ago, we got a call from a bank about a possible engagement. The president had apparently gone out and looked at a bank that had very good MIS productivity in all the branches. He then came back and called in his top MIS guy and gave him a rash of trouble because he thought they fell short by comparison.

Someone referred them to us and I went and met with their MIS person in San Francisco. Well, this guy wanted us to make a PC-based productivity tool that would tell them their productivity was good. I remember saying, "You want us to do what?" I had to tell him what we could do, which was an actual analysis of productivity and recommendations for improvement. But no, that's not what he wanted. He just wanted something to get the president off his back.

I told him you've got the wrong company. Well, he couldn't believe I would say that. He thought maybe we just couldn't construct the right kind of model. I said, "No, you don't understand. We do models all the time. But we only build honest models." With that I packed up my bag and left.

I had another incident like that. We had just done a major restructuring for a large finance company and toward the end of the engagement one of our principals reported he'd been contacted by another large finance company. I thought, great, they probably heard what we did and now they want our help.

I went to this meeting and there were four or five guys in the room. I got everybody's name but I didn't quite know everybody's position. Well, as the meeting went on I found myself thinking, "Jeez, I thought these guys were decision makers. They're acting like a bunch of people five levels down, asking me all kinds of inappropriate questions."

"Hmm, what would Satan do?"

They wanted to know exactly what I did for their competitor. Of course, I couldn't discuss that and told them so. They responded by saying, what do you mean you can't discuss that? If you want to work for us, then you'd better tell us what you did for them. I made it clear that wasn't going to happen. What we would be happy to do was evaluate their network, tell them the most efficient way to set it up.

They were indignant. I had to end the meeting. When I got outside, I said to my guy, "What were we in this meeting for? I thought these were decision makers."

He said, "That was the president throwing those questions at you." I couldn't believe that. I couldn't believe they would ask us those kinds of questions.

CARL LOBUE

Integrity Isn't a Luxury

If I were stupid enough to think that I could do ill or do wrong and get away with it for long, well, I'd be very naive and reveal my inexperience in the ways of the world. As a consultant, you may sometimes make an honest error of judgment and give a client advice that turns out to be bad or wrong. You try, in good conscience, to give the best advice you can. That's the only way to survive.

But giving the best advice you can at that time and not being right is a very different thing from deliberately giving poor advice because you think it is what the client wants to hear. An opportunist will be seen through quickly. Integrity isn't a luxury. It's a business necessity for survival. When the truth begins to be seen, opportunism will ruin a person. There's no future in giving less than your best honest advice.

Recently, in retirement, I had a very interesting experience. I'm officially a member of an advisory council to the Secretary of the Air Force Office of Public Affairs. They've been taking me around the country, letting me see some of their operations and their problems. It's marvelously interesting. They took me down to Kirkland Air Force Base in Texas where the Air Force gives basic training to the volunteers.

During training, the drill sergeant is with these recruits from morning to night for the first six weeks of their basic training. He has total authority over their lives until they become full members of the Air Force. While I was down there, a sergeant told me that when he calls the recruits out for reveille at 5 o'clock in the morning, as they are moving into formation, sometimes he might notice one of them scratching his face. He waits until they are all lined up at attention and then he hollers out, "All right, the man who scratched his face, fall out." He said they never do. Never once did anyone ever step forward.

So then, he points to the recruit who scratched his face. "You, fall out." And the kid is terrified. What is the drill sergeant going to do to him? And he says to him, "I don't care whether you scratched your face or not. It makes no difference to me. But I care that you lied. Don't you ever lie again. The lives of these other men depend on you telling them the truth and your life depends on them telling you the truth. Don't you ever lie again."

The sergeant said "That's how I make my point and the new airmen never forget it."

Sooner or later, the lack of ethical standards catches up with you. Lying or telling half-truths will destroy the future for a management consultant as well as for anybody else. I'm not preaching from the mountaintop about high-and-mighty ethical standards. I'm talking pragmatic, down-to-earth reality.

CHESTER BURGER

Who Wants That Kind of Person In His or Her Firm?

I've seen people trying to shop relationships: "If I join your firm, I will bring clients with me." These aren't common breaches, but you see them. I think if a client wants you to continue to serve them, then its fine. But it's very different from setting your own market value based on the client base that you could pull away from the firm. Because clients are not individual clients; the client is the firm. And if you're going to do that going in, you're going to do it going out. So who wants that kind of person in the firm?

EDWARD PRINGLE

Hmmm, What's This About?

Several years ago, I called on a major bank in California. I was talking to an executive vice president about what we did and how we did it. Well, he wanted to know if we ever worked as subcontractors. I said no, we never have, but we would if we thought it was appropriate. He then told me that all the consulting work for his bank was done through a subcontractor. I thought, hmm, okay, what's this about?

I felt uneasy about the arrangement so I never went to meet the contractor. But I'll be damned if about a year later this guy didn't get caught. He was running all the consulting business through a phony company, taking 10 percent off the top for himself. We're talking about something like $25 million worth of consulting work every year.

CARL LOBUE

The Interview Is Over

I think a bad apple gets thrown out very quickly. I've looked at statements and values of the number of consulting firms and integrity is always one of those value statements. At my firm, the statement of values begins with "We value integrity above all." It's the number one statement and it's a non-negotiable. And I think that is fundamental to any good consulting firm. Integrity can't be defined. It's one of those things you know when you see it and when you don't see it, you get the people out of there very, very fast.

There will be mistakes in every big firm. There will be some people who don't adhere to the value system but they should be weeded out ruthlessly and quickly. And I think in most cases they are.

I can remember a person I was interviewing who gave me a writing sample. It was a strategic plan that he had developed for a competitor. He was offering to leave it with me. My answer was real clear, "You take that and the interview is over. I don't have a decision to make, it's over."

I recall another time when I was interviewing a consultant. I asked him for the assignment that he was most proud of. And he said, "We had a client who wanted this computer system in their operations and they didn't want to add a single employee and we did that. They are fully computerized and they didn't add a single employee."

I said, "How are they going to maintain the system?"

"That's the beauty," he said. "They don't have a clue as to what's in that system so any time there's a change they have to hire us."

And again I said, "The interview's over." I don't think he ever understood why. It was a complete breach of reasonable judgment on how to serve a client.

EDWARD PRINGLE

Act on the Road the Way I Act at Home

I always want to act on the road the way I act at home. At home, I don't go to five-star restaurants, so if I'm on the road, I don't go to a five-star restaurant. At home, I'll have a very basic lunch and I'll take maybe half an hour for it. So on the road, I take a half-hour lunch and eat something quick. When I'm on vacation, I stay at a moderate hotel, so when I'm on the road, I do the same.

STEVE GOLDFIELD

Number One, I Try to Do Unto Others

Number one, I try to do unto others. I don't lie or steal. Of course, we all have professional standards of ethics. We have them in every professional association. But I don't look at ethics just in that light. I mean, it's nice to have a document. But I look at the standards issue as a very personal thing. Integrity is saying yes when you mean yes, and no when you mean no. I try to live that and sometimes it's very difficult to do that and be a consultant.

ALISON JACKSON

GOOD BUSINESS

It's Just Good Business to Be Honest

I always remind our people, you're only as good as your last job. You know we're not McKinsey. We can't screw up and come back to market and get a $5 million contract. In a service business such as ours, you're only as good as your last job. You always have to do a good job, be truthful and aboveboard. It's hard enough to get things done right when you're honest. If you've got to keep covering up lies, there's no way that's going to work. No one's clever enough to always cover his or her tracks. It's just good business to be honest with people and do things right.

When you work overseas, you are going to run into situations where people routinely make payoffs to get work. I won't get involved in that. If we can't do the work legitimately, then we don't want it. Frankly, it's going to bite you in the rear sooner or later. You only need one circumstance like that to ruin your reputation forever. It's never worth it.

CARL LOBUE

The Accusation Is Going to Be on the Front Page

In general, we are going to have access to certain sensitive information, like marketing strategies and the like. Anyone who violates that kind of confidentiality probably should be tied to the stake and burned. All you need is one instance of confidentiality being violated to tarnish your firm. Of course, the accusation is going to be on the front page, but if it turns out not to be true, the retraction will be way back on page 18.

WILLARD ARCHIE

"Made it in six. Billed them for seven."

The Only Thing We Have in This Business Is Our Reputation

When you think about it, the only thing we really have in this business is our reputation. If you lose that, you don't have a consulting firm.

ALAN ANDOLSEN

Honesty Is the Best Policy

In general, honesty is the best policy. It's a long-term business, and somebody who's dishonest cannot survive long-term.

More specifically, I look at the level of intellectual dishonesty, rather than an out-and-out lie. Intellectual dishonesty means, is that really the best advice you can give to your client, or are you just trying to sell add-on work or the next job? That's intellectually dishonest. That is a very short-term gain.

My belief and that of my firm is that by and large, if you give the best advice you can give, that is in the client's best interest. And over time, if you do that well, your interests will follow those of the clients.

You have the ultimate weapon and that is you can simply dissolve the relationship. I've pulled the plug on a number of major assignments because we really couldn't work with the client. And the pain of doing that, depending on how far into it you are, is huge. You've got stuff you haven't billed, or stuff you've billed but you haven't been paid. All of that gets put at risk.

But on the other hand, it's necessary if you're going to be intellectually honest with yourself and your team. A partner and I were talking about a project. I was the client partner and I showed up about two weeks into my colleague's assignment and spent three days doing a review. The third night was the big dinner with the project team. And this was a big assignment in those days. This was a multi-million dollar deal at a time when if you got over seven figures you were doing well. I went around the table, and there were probably twenty people at the table, and I asked each one of them individually, do you think that we can be successful in meeting the client's expectations under the current conditions?

And I got 100 percent "no"s. I said, well, this tells me that we ought to pull the plug. It was one of those things where the client was supposed to be taking actions but they hadn't moved, and we were getting further and further behind.

So the next morning we pulled the plug and packed it up. Now, the short-term hit was big. I think the short-term hit was a million and a half bucks, which was pretty big numbers back in the '70s. Over the next six months, we renegotiated the project and the relationship. And six months of renegotiations costs you a lot of money, too.

And here we are 25 years later, and the total revenue from that client in those 25 years is past 100 million dollars. So you know, we took the right action, but in the short term, it was very painful. We got the relationship reinitiated on the basis in which the client's expectations could be met in a way that we judged successful. And the relationship is still there today.

ANONYMOUS A

We All Make Good Money

I knew a guy who claimed that it's easy to fudge on your expense reports that you can get a receipt and use it in a lot of different ways. You can rebook a flight multiple times and receive for each flight and just keep charging those through and nobody can really tell. And because expenses are always passed through at cost, there's less of a screen on what you spent than would be otherwise.

So I guess you could cheat if you wanted to. But I'd say that the number of people who actually do or did that is like one percent, or even less than one percent. I mean, we all make good money. Faking expenses is a really stupid way to lose your main source of income because you're going to make an extra 100 bucks or whatever the hell it was on your expense report. It's just stupid.

In the long term, you just can't get away with being a slime ball.

JAMES BLOMBERG

A Nice Companion

I've seen situations where some individuals, usually new to the consultant business, decide that perhaps an employee or client might make a nice companion over the six months or however long they're on a project. I've also never seen it work out well. Our company approach has been that this sort of thing shouldn't happen—definitely a no-no. When it starts to become obvious, then maybe it's time for reassignments to be made. I've never seen a client who was happy when this happens, either. It's pretty much a relationship killer. If you're the person doing it, you just better be very influential in your company, so you still have a job when the assignment's over.

COBY FRAMPTON

CLIENT INTERESTS VS. CONSULTANT INTERESTS

The Interest of the Client vs. the Interest of the Firm

It seems to me the biggest ethical issue that most consultants deal with is the interest of the client versus the interest of the firm. And increasingly that involves the ownership of intellectual property. That's the biggest issue.

The second biggest issue deals with conflicts of interest. I got sued once for not taking a consulting assignment with a client who wanted my services. I said I have a relationship with a direct competitor and I can't take your assignment. And they tried to sue me. They argued that as a public accountant I was failing to hold myself available for the public. I actually got a lawyer's letter on that and it was very quickly thrown out.

But I do think that is one of the real challenges in today's world – who you can serve. Realistically, how do you build barriers in a firm the size of the largest consulting firms today? You can't just serve one client per industry. You can't just serve non-competing clients.

I think an awful lot goes back not to systems but to the basic integrity of the consultant. Consultants have to understand when there's a conflict. And they have to protect their clients' interests. I think they do an awfully good job of this. Better certainly than legal and investment banking and other areas that might be compared to consulting.

EDWARD PRINGLE

There Is a Tension Between Telling the Truth and Solving Problems

I prided myself on being the truth teller. In the final analysis, I'm not sure it was always the most effective means of communicating on some tough issues. I remember getting a couple of clients really upset to the point that on one occasion my boss literally had to leap in and take over the presentation. I remember him being very angry, and sitting across the aisle on the plane back home and not speaking with me. Then, as we waited for our luggage at the airport, he came over to me and said, "Just remember, if your client wants to jump out the window, your job is to help him up onto the window sill."

I've never forgotten that bad advice. It presents a fundamental question about the consultant's obligation but I'm glad I heard it early in my career. It made a big difference in how I thought about myself in relation to the profession. It's obviously advice I didn't take, but at the core it has a very thorny real life problem, and that's that things are not reducible so quickly and easily as to always be able to tell the truth.

For example, we had undertaken a turnaround study for a large industrial company to figure out what would be the most economically beneficial way to get them out of a business that one of the divisions was in. There were about five different ways to get out of the business, and we calculated the after-tax consequences of each and made a presentation as to what the five alternatives were. The study was a great success, beyond the client's expectations. And the chairman, who was not the person who hired us to do the study, was terribly impressed with the piece of work.

About three or four months later, as we were implementing that study, he asked to see me. He asked if I would take on a personal assignment, not as part of a team but as an individual consultant. And what he said was that he was terribly concerned with the performance of his immediate subordinates. He anecdotally explained what he was disappointed in, and said he wasn't quite sure what to do about the problem because it was kind of pervasive. It wasn't one or two people who might be replaced. He was very concerned about his whole second tier. So he asked me to look into it, see what the problem was, evaluate it, and make some recommendations. I was pleased to be asked to deal with such a sensitive matter, and I was complimented that the chairman of a major corporation would look to me to do that kind of work.

I spent a couple of months looking at the problem and reached the conclusion privately that the problem wasn't his immediate subordinates—he was the problem. I sat down to think through the recommendations and I had a crisis regarding whether I should tell him the truth or not. If the client wants to jump out the window, do I help him up to the sill? Certainly one can always find some fault in any subordinate. None of us are perfect, but in terms of the systematic problem he was describing, he was the problem.

But the problem was pretty straightforward. If I tell this guy that he's the problem, that's going to be the end of my relationship. He won't have the capacity to take any criticism. In the end, I decided that the higher ethical calling was to tell the client the truth. I proceeded to draft a 16-page report to the client and to this day, in terms of the quality of writing, I think it's the finest piece of work I've ever done. It was well-crafted, it was tactful, it was direct but diplomatic, it explained a lot and took him off the hook but in the end, made it quite clear that he was the problem, that he had to address certain issues and forces within himself. And that was the last time I had any contact with that client.

Not too long after that, there was an unfriendly takeover of the company. While some people got out with money, it was just a matter of time before every last employee lost his or her job. For more than a decade after that

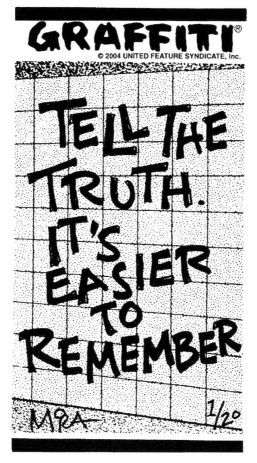

Graffiti: © United Feature Syndicate, Inc.

I kept asking myself, did I do the right thing? And for the better part of a decade I said yeah, it's always best to tell the truth. And it was only later that I came to think that that was not the case. This man didn't have the capacity to hear the truth, and if I couldn't solve the problem he would never rely on another consultant again. So in a sense, I had the last opportunity to try to effect change. And in telling the truth, I surrendered any chance of being a force for change within the enterprise.

I finally understood that the opposite of telling the truth was not to tell a lie, but rather it was rather to be effective in bringing about change. That the issue wasn't truth or lack thereof but rather how can I be potent, how can I be effective. In retrospect, there were probably some things that I could and might and should have done other than simply point out that he was the source of the problem. I could have hung around long enough to try to work through the problem because I don't think you solve those kinds of problems overnight. Somebody had to hang in there to try and work through it.

You grapple over what is the obligation of the consultant, what is your responsibility. There's a tension between telling the truth and solving problems. And those are not always synonymous.

CARL SLOANE

My Son Is Not Going to Be President?

When I first joined the firm I learned a good lesson. We were doing a study of a paper converter here in Chicago. The company had two owners. The chairman was an inventor, and he developed machinery for converting paper, and for making decorative paper and ribbons and bows. His partner was the president; he was a salesperson. The third player was the chairman's son, who was the vice president of marketing.

Our task was to do a complete review of the business. They were having trouble. The chairman was about 75, the president perhaps 70. They were trying to think about what they should do with the business after they retire. We did all the interviews and analysis and we interviewed the son.

We concluded that the son was absolutely unqualified to be the vice president of marketing. He was a physics teacher from a Chicago high school who they brought into the business because his father and the president had decided that they were eventually going to leave the business.

They wanted to see if they could leave it to the son. By the way, he reported not to his father but to the president.

Once we got the whole thing laid out we said, "Boy, we've got to tell the chairman that his son's not qualified to be president. In fact, he's not qualified to be vice president of marketing. In fact, he should go back and teach school." He had no qualifications whatsoever to be in this business.

So we said to ourselves, "How do we say this? Do we sugarcoat it somehow? If we tell the old man, he's going to be really, really upset." Finally we put together a very high level report that included what had to be done to revitalize the business, how the company should be organized, and the issue of the son. We had the meeting on top of the Prudential building, which was then the tallest building in Chicago. We were looking out over the lake, as we made the presentation.

Finally we get to the part about the son. This is the organization and this is the way it should be structured. And when we talked about the son, the president asked if he would be a good successor. We all said "No," in unison so that no single consultant would be exposed. "Well, he's really not qualified. He doesn't have his heart in it. He really should go back teaching physics."

The father said, "So you mean my son is not going to be the new president?" We said yes. He said, "That's the best goddamned news I ever heard! This nincompoop," he added, "if we ever put him in here as president, I would sell my share in this company in a heart beat!"

Well, the president looked at him and said, "I thought you were the one pushing him for this."

"No," the chairman replied, "I thought you were the one who liked him and was pushing him." They start to talk to each other, and it comes out that neither one thought the son was qualified. They each thought that the other person did, and that the other was pushing him to be president. And we're looking at one another and I'm saying to myself, well, that's a lesson to learn early in your career.

You don't fool around. You don't make up answers. You tell the truth. And that turns out to be the best policy. Honesty is the best policy in consulting.

RAYMOND EPICH

Am I Going to Anger the Client Who Pays the Bills?

I'm trying to deal with the consulting side versus the CPA side because there are whole different sets of rules. If I uncover questionable situations, I am bound to deal appropriately with them. The question is how do you do it and with whom? Of course, the first thing you have to do is verify the facts. Then there are certain choices. I'll go to the Board of Directors or other leadership if I think some inappropriate action has taken place. It's tough. After all, these are the people paying our bills. Am I going to anger the client who pays the bills?

For the consultant, the issue is not necessarily legal versus illegal. I had a case where we uncovered some highly questionable expenditures, and mob connections were suspected. But I don't know that they were necessarily illegal. We run into a lot of situations that involve shades of gray, as opposed to matters of legality.

Frankly, if you're in this business long enough, you're going to run into all kinds of crap, some of which may involve legal issues. As a CPA firm, we have to be absolutely clear. If a client will not do something according to Generally Accepted Accounting Principles, then we will resign the account. Period! We don't have a choice. You can be sure that most of the bad stuff will come out at some point. I'm absolutely sure of that.

WILLARD ARCHIE

You Have to Be Up Front With Clients

What I believe is that you have to be up front with clients. If they ask you to do X, and you've never done X, but it sounds like an area you'd like to get into, do you say, of course we'll go ahead and do this work? Or do you say, we'd love to team with you on this, but we don't have much experience here?

If they say, well, you've never done this type of project before, no thanks, then we'll just move on. But 98 percent of the time the response is okay, let's work on it. The clients are usually glad we've told them where we're at. The attitude is that this can be a learning experience for all of us. Of course, they will expect some consideration in pricing. But if you're building a new practice base and somebody's paying you for it, that's not such a bad deal.

ALAN ANDOLSEN

No Free Lunches

The ethical question that I've seen more of involves people in a position to make decisions who look for gifts or some kind of reward if they give you the business. I know sometimes it has hurt our business because we don't do that. Sometimes they'll be very straightforward and say, "Well, you're bidding against XYZ Company." They'll let you know it might be in your interest to throw in something extra. Our policy is if we have to do this kind of thing to get business, then we're probably doing something wrong. So let's not do it, particularly when somebody just comes right out and asks for something. I think you'll find it's not an uncommon occurrence in large companies.

Some companies have recognized the problem and put in place strict rules on what can and cannot be done. No free lunches. We have a number of clients who are adamant about vendors and consultants not offering them any gifts. Consequently, I probably get more free lunches from clients than I take clients to lunch.

COBY FRAMPTON

I Stayed In the Hotel Room

There's a great potential for conflict of interest for all firms that have more than one service line. We do economic development consulting in addition to our location consulting business. Sometimes potential sites would offer us a development project, on the condition that they were chosen to get a plant. We would always say that's not how it's done.

But that was the most obvious and the most common occurrence. Sometimes you'd find a bottle of wine in a hotel and some fruit, but that was fairly innocuous. At what point is it a bribe and at what point is it just an attempt to be gracious? But if you got an offer to go off to a party, well, it was pretty obvious what was going on. I stayed in the hotel and read and read.

FORD HARDING

You Have to Believe What You're Selling

If you put your client's interests first, what does that mean in terms of taking risks with clients on new ideas? You know there's going to be some risk there. But is it unethical or unprofessional if you have a deep conviction that this is where the industry's going? You should go out and convince the client, dare I say sell the client on that idea.

You have to believe what you're selling. But that's a very personal decision. You have to do due diligence on what is a new value proposition. You may think, I haven't done this work, but I can get a couple of my partners to come in and work with me. I think I can learn how to do it, and I do think it's right for the client. And I don't think anybody else can deliver it any more cheaply than we can.

You just have to have some objectivity and guts about it on both sides. And I think that if you ignore your objective conclusion, then you're being unprofessional. I'm not sure where the line is between unprofessional and unethical, but it's pretty thin. I suppose a lot of salesmen sell people things they don't really believe they need. Some people say that's smart, other people say it's unethical. I'm not sure it's either one, just self-serving.

The spectrum of ethical behavior is pretty broad in consulting firms, although it's probably not much different than it is in other industries. Whether you're selling chicken to restaurants or corporate strategy studies to big oil companies, you still have to ask yourself, am I putting my client's interest first? If you sell a bad chicken, you're going to lose the customer.

An interesting question is whether bad ethical behavior is punished more or less promptly in consulting compared to other industries. And from what I've seen, it is certainly not punished more promptly. There's a lot of tolerance for bad behavior. And that tolerance seems to go along with ability to get clients.

BILL MATASSONI

The Data Need to Speak

Consulting involves dealing with people's jobs, internal politics, all sorts of sensitive issues. I had an engagement with a fairly good-sized bank, for example, where their IT organization was just not cutting it. When we looked at the organization structure we found the CIO was very ineffective. It was a situation where no one wanted to upset the guy. So I walked into the chairman's office and just laid it out. I said, "You're not getting any value at all from the CIO, and as a matter of fact, he ought to leave." I mean, he was literally taking naps in the afternoon in the office. He was just of no value.

The chairman asked for my recommendation about how to handle it. I said, "This guy is close to retirement, just buy him out, give him a retirement package." His response was, "Wow, this guy! We can't do anything with him." I said "We should take that as a challenge." Not only was he not adding any value, he was holding them back. I suggested they start to put a couple of people in place to fill his role. We could help with putting the right skills in place.

We had to work with the chairman over a six-week period until he was ready to do this. Then we helped put a retirement package together, and they were able to let the guy go. He was not as direct as I would have liked, but within a year to a year and a half, the guy was out of the organization.

My take on things is that the data need to speak, but on the other hand you have a lot of people involved, and for the most part people have a very difficult time disrupting or ending someone else's career. I would say the profession does a pretty good job of making sure that the data speaks. But then you have to get realistic on the implementation, and that involves individuals.

MICHAEL ALBRECHT

Do You Give Somebody a Can of Coke?

There's a movie called *Doc Hollywood* with Michael J. Fox, where he's on his way to Los Angeles. He's this young, sharp whippersnapper from out East, heading out to LA to be a doctor at a big hospital. He gets lost, crashes into a fence in a small town and is sentenced to community service as their doctor a few weeks while their regular older doctor is unavailable.

And what happens is that somebody rushes in this little kid. He's turning blue and everything and the young doctor diagnoses this as some terrible thing, saying he has to operate right away and to send for the chopper and that he needs all this equipment.

The old doctor finally shows up and he looks at the kid. He gives him a can of Coke to drink. The kid drinks the Coke, belches and he's okay.

So the question is, as a consultant, do you give the client the most complex solution and complicate the situation, or do you give somebody a can of Coke?

ALEX ZABROSKY

Always Do the Right Thing

The most controversial thing I ever had to do was to fire the whole managing executive board of a client here in the Netherlands. I was hired by the supervisory board, which is a non-executive oversight body, to review the executive board's performance. It was actually their own job to do, but they handed it off to me.

I did my interviews and research and found myself coming to the difficult conclusion that the three executive directors on the board were in fact not functioning at all. The chairman was terrible; nobody could mention anything that he had ever done. Most of the people didn't even know him. The other two members were functioning just as poorly. I thought they all had to go.

This caused me an enormous dilemma, and for good reason. Any recommendations regarding the executive board would entail a royal decision signed by the Queen. This particular institution had a national charter. So my recommendation would have to be approved by the appropriate minister, verified by parliament, and then signed by the Queen.

So there I was, the simple consultant, about to recommend that the chairman and the executive board be fired. As you might imagine, I really had to weigh my decision carefully. I must have spent three weeks considering and reconsidering my recommendation. I did talk to some of my colleagues, but I was pretty much on my own on this one. The chairman of the supervisory board was also a weak manager so he was very happy to put it all on me. But I knew what I had to do. This institution would never be a success as long as they were there.

The next step was to go to the minister. Well, the last thing you need is a top civil servant who says to you, you're crazy and that's impossible. And that's exactly what I got. I had to tell him, "Well, maybe I am crazy but it took me weeks to come to this conclusion. And right now I am very, very serious about it. It must be done this way."

There was another potential problem. I was very afraid that when I told the board they had to go, it would be all over the media. And that in turn would cause questions in parliament and you can imagine what else. Fortunately, the minister decided he would accept my advice. He gave me the green light and at 10 o'clock the next morning I spoke to the chairman, at ten thirty to the second man, and by 11 o'clock to the third. By noon we had held a meeting with the supervisory board and by two o'clock in the afternoon they were all fired. And by two thirty the work council, parliament, and the local press had all been informed.

This turned out to be one of my most sensational assignments. There was tremendous news coverage of the story. Fortunately, everyone who knew about the situation was convinced that this was good advice. In fact, just recently I met the man who was then chairman of the supervisory board and he still says, wise decision, you did a good job.

But you never know if that will be the outcome, until that moment when you tell them what your advice is. That's what makes this work so exciting. Will I survive or have I committed career suicide? And so perhaps the moral of the story, in a Calvinist sort of way, is always do the right thing. Do your job. Be absolutely honest and convinced and never do something because you're counting on a certain type of reaction. Do it because you are absolutely convinced that this is the right advice. Even if everybody keeps telling you that you should do something different. Hopefully, you will leave convinced that your contribution has added something.

GEERT VAN DEE

Are You Practicing Ethical Behavior in Your Business?

The following 12 general principles make up the key elements of conduct in the consulting business. They were developed for the Association of Management Consulting Firm by the Code of Ethics Committee of the same organization, led by Alan Andolsen, former Committee Chairman.

Andolsen notes, "You could look at our industry code of ethics as a form of self-policing. We are honor bound to report violations of the code is we observe them. But it is more than self-policing. There is an educational element for both consultants and potential clients. We want to get the word out there are principles, and whether you hire an association firm or not, here is what you should be looking for as far as qualifications."

Whether you follow these principles in your work as a consultant, or use them as a guideline in selecting a consulting firm to work with your company, these 12 principles set a very high standard indeed.

Code of Ethics - Association of Management Consulting Firms

The Code of Ethics assures the users of consulting services that AMCF members are publicly committed to providing the highest quality work. Member firms subscribe to this Code of Ethics or maintain a substantially similar Code of Ethics.

CLIENTS

1. We will serve our clients with integrity, competence, and objectivity.

2. We will keep client information and records of client engagements confidential and will use proprietary client information only with the client's permission.

3. We will not take advantage of confidential client information for ourselves.

4. We will not disclose to our clients any conflicts of interest of which we are aware before undertaking an engagement.

ENGAGEMENTS

5. We will accept only engagements for which we are qualified by our experience and competence.

6. We will assign staff to client engagements in accord with their experience, knowledge, and expertise.

7. We will immediately acknowledge any influences on our objectivity to our clients and will offer to withdraw from a consulting engagement when our objectivity or integrity may be impaired.

FEES

8. We will agree independently and in advance with our clients on the basis for our fees and expenses and will charge fees and expenses that are reasonable, legitimate, and commensurate with the services we deliver and the responsibility we accept.

9. We will disclose to our clients in advance any fees or commissions that we expect to receive for equipment, supplies or services we recommend to our clients.

PROFESSION

10. We will respect the intellectual property rights of our clients, other consulting firms, and sole practitioners and will not use proprietary information or methodologies without permission.

11. We will not advertise our services in a deceptive manner and will not misrepresent the consulting profession, consulting firms, or sole practitioners.

12. We will encourage reporting of violations of this Code of Ethics by member firms to the AMCF Board of Directors.

-7-

On the Road Again: The Traveling Consultant

"Well, my dad is kind of like a migrant worker."

COBY FRAMPTON'S 6-YEAR-OLD SON

This chapter begins where most consultants often begin their week—pondering how much time they're going to spend on the road before they can return home. There's a lot to ponder, too. One consultant tells us he figures over the course of his career he's slept a total of 12 years in hotels. Another has accumulated enough miles to circle the globe a few times over, or fly to the moon and back a couple of times. That's the world of the modern consultant, a never-ending story of life on the road.

What's life like for the traveling consultant? It's about days that begin at airports and end in strange cities in different time zones and unfamiliar hotel rooms. It's about the quirkiness of small towns and locals who like to put cream on every pie in their municipality. Or airline flights where pilot, baggage handler, security guard, and flight attendant are one and the same person. It's about surviving earthquakes and cabdrivers who don't know if Delaware is on the way to Philadelphia and—being a consultant used to solving problems—thinking you can drive through the worst snowstorm in recent history.

In this chapter we learn about the tedium and the tension and the moments when you get a little past sanity on your way to somewhere. But we also learn about the exhilaration and the great variety of experiences and people you can encounter along the way. Mostly, perhaps, we come to appreciate the consultant's motto to at all cost, "Just keep moving."

As our mostly veteran contributors reveal, making it all work and staying sane requires discipline. Here we discover the variety of rules, tips, and practices consultants develop to help them survive life on the road. Consultants often become masters of the perks and upgrades and hotel deals and frequent flyer miles and every possible advantage they can finagle to make life on the road more pleasant. That may be no small matter, either, in these days increasing flight delays, more seats and shorter leg room on planes, and heightened security measures. Not to mention just the sheer increase in numbers of air travelers.

If travel is the bane of our existence, it is also the source of much of the flavor and allure of our business. Yes, it's a bizarre life. But it's also an interesting life.

I'M SORRY, SIR, BUT HE'S OUT OF
TOWN THIS WEEK (AND NEXT)

Close to 10 Million Miles

I don't know for sure how many miles I've flown. It must be over three million miles on American, two million on United, and I've got gold cards on five or six other airlines. I can tell you our vacations have all been on free mileage. I have six kids and the five oldest all flew back and forth to college at least a couple times a semester for free. In fact, not only do my kids come to me for free tickets, but they'll ask me if I've got tickets for their friends, too. I imagine I've probably had hundreds of free tickets, and accumulated close to 10 million miles over the last 15 years.

CARL LOBUE

12 Years In a Hotel

I was in the consulting business from 1969 through 1998, some 29 years. I worked in nearly 30 different states and probably 10 foreign countries. I figure I made at least one round trip per week or 50 per year. Over 29 years, this adds up to at least 1,500 or more round trips out of and back into O'Hare Airport. In total, I've flown over three million actual air miles.

Think about it this way: I spent an average of three nights per week away from home. Over 29 years, this works out to 4,500 nights, or over 12 complete years sleeping in a hotel. If you divide the three million miles by an average air speed of 500 mph, I spent some 6,000 hours in the air. This is the equivalent of 250 complete 24 hour days or three years of the average person's work week. This doesn't even include the time spent going to and from the airport, standing in ticket and security lines, and waiting in a queue for take off which would easily double the totals.

And you know what? I wouldn't have missed any of it.

RICHARD METZLER

The 'Migrant Worker'

When my son was six years old, his teacher kept him in from recess one day because she thought he was having problems. It seemed that every time the teacher discussed something in class that dealt with any kind of manufacturing industry or product, my son would say, "My dad does that." If the teacher later brought up another industry or product, my son would say, "My dad does that, too."

Well, finally the teacher had had enough of this. She kept him after recess for a little talk. "Now, Brandon, I know you're proud of what your father does," she said. But you can't keep telling these stories. He can't possibly be doing all these things I talk about in class. Now, tell me, what does he really do?"

You have to picture this six year old sitting there. He thought for a minute and then he said, "Well, he's kind of like a migrant worker." Actually, that's what I would tell him, I was like a migrant worker. And that's really how it looked to him. I was always traveling, working at one place or another, bringing souvenirs home. In fact, if I was expected home, it became kind of a ritual in our family for the kids to stay up to see what I'd manage to bring back. Of course, they'd be disappointed with certain clients, like the one who made surgical instruments. Then it would be, "Thanks, but no thanks."

COBY FRAMPTON

And Bring Your Seat to the Upright Position

As I was completing an 18-month project that required commuting weekly from Chicago to Houston, my wife and I went to a movie. Upon sitting down in the theater, with its cushioned seat and the blank screen up front, I instinctively reached for the seat belt.

Not surprisingly, at the end of that same 18-month project in Houston, the airline and hotel staff all knew me by name. But I was definitely surprised when, as my wife and I were en route to a client party at the project's conclusion, the Avis shuttle driver called to me by my first name as I got on the bus.

ROBERT ARNOLD

Surviving the First Months

The first three months are probably the worst. There is definitely a lot of adjustment. But very few of our consultants have quit because of the travel. We find it takes about 18 months before they either can't stand the travel or they're fine with it and they're going to stay. If they can get past those first 18 months, they'll usually stay with it for a very long time, maybe until they retire. Last year two people left because of the travel. They'd been on the road roughly two years.

CYNTHIA DRISKILL

THE OCCASIONAL CLOSE CALL

Neither Sleet nor Rain nor Dead Geese
Shall Keep You From Your Appointed Rounds

My plane hit a goose taking off from LaGuardia going to Dulles. We had to get to the airport during rush hour so we had left a little early. Well, we got there in plenty of time and ended up taking an early flight. Then the plane hits the goose, we go off the runway, and they abort the flight. Fortunately, we had not been wheels up or we probably would be dead. In the end, we ended up on the flight we were originally scheduled on.

MIKE LAPORTA

When the Pilot Has a Hot Date

I recall flying in from an interview in Cleveland to Newark one night and visibility was very bad. I remember it so clearly because unfortunately that was the night a plane went down on Long Island and crashed. It was in a holding pattern and ran out of fuel. That same night I was on a plane in a holding pattern. It was a scary experience because we were circling for quite some time. In fact, the lady next to me was white as a ghost. I really thought she was going to get sick. I remember using any kind of humor I could to keep her mind off of things. If you think I was being kind, I also didn't want her to throw up on me, so there was something in it for me.

Actually, there was so much turbulence I was terrified. It was like being stuck on an amusement park ride for an hour. You just felt like there was no floor. As the plane was coming down for its final descent, the engines slowed down, and then all of a sudden just cranked up and we shot straight up. I don't know how the pilot could see anything. There was just no visibility. The pilot then came on informing us that we had just run out of runway. We had shot too far over. The tower was now reporting visibility below the legal limit. We were going to be on an indefinite hold until we either got reassigned or got another crack at landing. Or maybe ran out of fuel.

I had the uneasy feeling that maybe the pilot had a hot date in Newark that night. I mean, how could it be clear to land one minute and not the next? I'm sure the visibility was not at the level where it should have been on the first approach. Obviously, he couldn't see the runway. This was not a good feeling.

Eventually we ended up being diverted to Syracuse. After landing I overheard the pilot remark to one of the flight attendants about "the close call we had back there." I think we had the option later that night to try to fly back, but I decided to stay overnight. The last thing my wife had heard was that I was going into Newark from Cleveland. Then she heard that a flight went down but she didn't know where. So she was pretty uptight until I called her and told her where I was.

And where I intended to stay until things improved.

TERRY GALLAGHER

"Food! Food!"

Trains, Planes, and Earthquakes

Remember the Steve Martin and John Candy film, Trains, Planes, and Automobiles? I think we've all been there. You're trying to get home to see the family for the weekend and its one calamity after another. All of us have to get very adept at sleeping in airports, enduring canceled flights, snowstorms and being stuck at O'Hare when the electricity goes out because of a thunderstorm. There's no way around it. Travel is the bane of our existence.

Most of my experience has not been too exciting. But I did go through an earthquake while working on a project in Los Angeles. This was back in the '70s. It was the middle of the night and I was sound asleep. I remember waking up, feeling very disoriented. I could hear splashing water in the toilet and said to myself, why is the water sloshing back and forth? I wasn't sure what was going on. All of a sudden it felt like someone just lifted the building up and dropped it. You can bet that woke me up! My mind was suddenly very clear, and there was one word in it—earthquake! I thought, what am I supposed to do? Okay, I know, I'll go stand in the doorway. So I ran over and stood in the doorway between the bedroom and the bathroom. But then I thought, wait a second, I'm on the 35th floor. If the building collapses, standing in this doorway is going to do me absolutely no good whatsoever. So, instead, I just went back to bed as the aftershocks rolled through. Somehow I survived.

DAVID TIERNO

Always Prepared

Less than a year after going through an earthquake in Mexico, I found myself in Los Angeles in a hotel. I had just finished with some nice room service and was sitting down having that last cup of coffee before my meeting when all of a sudden I looked out the window and the water was coming out of the hotel swimming pool. Then my coffee cup started shaking and the toilet fell off the wall. It was one of those toilets that was hung on the wall, rather than on the floor.

Later that year I was in Washington, D.C., to pitch a client the next day. I was there the evening before and was planning to get some sleep before the meeting the next morning. The client had brought in some people from out of town, who were also staying at the same hotel. It must have been about one o'clock in the morning when there was this terrible knocking on my door. Someone was yelling, the hotel's on fire, you've got to get out.

Being a heavy sleeper I started debating with the guy about whether I had to leave or not. He convinced me I should leave. I got downstairs where I found the rest of my team. We ended up having the meeting we were going to have right in the lobby. In the end, I think it helped us win the job. You could say we had two chances at orals, so to speak.

Of course, now I always keep at least one change of clothes right there ready to jump into. That way if I have to evacuate, at least I can do so looking crisp.

MIKE LAPORTA

CONSULTANT'S MOTTO: ALWAYS KEEP MOVING

Stupid Is As Stupid Does

My favorite story concerns the giant snowfall in 1967. Three of us were returning from a project with the Tennessee Valley Authority. Our plane had just landed in Indianapolis where we learned we couldn't go any further because O'Hare was snowed in. I was with two other consultants, Ev and Jack, and I remember saying to them, "Look, a lot of wimpy people are going to stay here in Indianapolis. But if you really want to get to Chicago, believe me, I'll show you how to get there. We're not stupid. We can do it. There's no such thing as a snowstorm you can't drive through."

My plan was to avoid driving up Highway 41 through Indiana. Instead, we would drive straight west from Indianapolis out to Route 66, which was then the main highway going southwest. Then we'd come in from the southwest and dodge all the snow. I managed to convince my partners that this would work, and we walked over to the Hertz counter. Ev was going to rent the car.

"We're going to Chicago and I want to rent a car," Ev told the Hertz agent. "Sorry sir," the agent told him, "we can't rent any autos to Chicago. There's too much snow." "Wait a minute," Ev said, "You don't know who I am. I'm a Vice President of a big consulting firm. I rent cars every week. I demand a car!" The agent held her ground. "Sorry, sir, but my orders are not to give out any cars to anybody."

Ev demanded to speak to her supervisor, to and he read him the riot act. Finally, they gave us a car, a map, and we were on our way. Now, this was a Thursday, about 5 or 6 o'clock in the evening. The snow was still piling up in Chicago, eventually some 28 inches. I remember Jack kept saying, "Why do we have to do this? Can't we just stay in a hotel here in Indianapolis and wait until the snow stops?" And I kept telling him, "Jack, listen, there's no such thing as a snow you can't drive through. We'll just go out to Route 66 and up into Chicago. Don't worry."

So we started driving west. It was pitch black and snowing like crazy. You can't imagine how much it was snowing. The road was like glass; it was so icy. We were only about two miles out of Indianapolis when we came to a bridge over a river. There was a truck on the bridge that had gone through the guardrail. It was just hanging over the side. This got Jack going again. "Can't we just turn around? Why do we have to do this?" "Jack, just shut up," I said, "We know what we're doing."

We finally got on a two-lane state road going west where we found ourselves behind a big truck. Ev was driving so I told him to stay behind the truck. We could keep our distance and just let the truck plow us through. By then the snow was really starting to get deep. We were already talking a foot on the highway. Shortly after we crossed into Illinois, the truck suddenly stopped, right on the road. So we stopped, too. We were maybe 20 feet behind the truck. It was about 8 o'clock in the evening and the snow was just coming down harder and harder. We could barely see a thing. I was thinking this truck driver was obviously a wimp. I was also wondering how we're going to get around him. Of course, we didn't really know what was going on. For all we knew, the truck was stuck behind someone, too.

I was designated to go out and see what was happening. I opened the door and the darned wind almost pulled the door off the car. I couldn't see a thing! No houses, no farms, nothing except this truck with its taillights. I climbed through snow that must have been two feet deep, wearing only a suit and topcoat, no muffler, no hat, no gloves. I got up to the truck and pounded on the window. This guy was just sitting there, staring out the window. He rolled the window down.

"What's up?" I asked him. "I can't go any further," he said. "It's just too deep." "You know, we're stuck behind you in our car." "Well, you can come on up here," he said. "I've got diesel fuel. I've got a lot of fuel—100 gallons. Hop in. I'll just lie in the back on the shelf. By the way," he added as if I needed reassuring, "don't worry, you can't get carbon monoxide poisoning from a diesel truck."

So I went back to the car and pounded on our window. "Okay, it's to the truck, boys. Let's go" and the three of us piled into the truck. The driver had a flare wedged between the dashboard and the gas pedal to keep it going a little more than idle. He climbed on the back shelf while Ev took the driver's seat. I was in the passenger seat and Jack was sitting on the floor in front of me. It was about 9:00 p.m. by then.

And there we sat, all night. All I did was stare out the window. You couldn't see a damn thing. It was nothing but blinding, blinding snow. Ev was the only one who seemed to sleep. The snow just kept coming down, blowing across these farm fields, never slowing down. Eventually it piled up to the cab roof. All this time there was nothing to eat; nothing to drink. The truck driver said he was going to Colorado and had a truck full of beer, but he couldn't touch it because it was all sealed and chained. Meanwhile, he was snacking back there on whatever he was going to eat in the first place. I guess we could have gone out and got some snow to munch on or some icicles. But we just stayed inside.

We stayed in that truck until about noon the next day. Of course, what was on everybody's mind through all this was my by now famous line: "There's no such thing as snowstorm you can't drive through." I had become highly quotable. It was Friday around noon before it finally began to clear up and the sun came out. Only then could we see where we were. There was a farmhouse just 300 or 400 feet off the road. And shortly after, this farmer came out with his giant tractor. It was one of these tractors with wheels about five feet high. He drove over and offered to take us into town.

Apparently, the farmer had known all along we were out there. He'd been keeping us under surveillance, he said, waiting for the snow to stop. By now the snow was probably up to our waists. The car was absolutely buried in snow. Luckily, it wasn't an ice storm so the car wasn't welded to the ground. The farmer put a chain on the front bumper of this brand new car and just dragged us around sideways like we were a sled. He pulled us all the way into this town called Leroy. It was near Rantoul somewhere. Mostly, it was just nowhere. There was a narrow path down the middle of Main Street and that's where he dropped us off. We thanked him and offered him some money, but he said no.

So there we were in Leroy. There was a saloon nearby so that's where we went. Obviously, we were very hungry. I ordered a double shot of scotch and a dried beef jerky thing hanging from the bar. Then it was back to the car and on our way to Route 66. Somehow we made it to Route 66. It was just a mess. Cars were in the ditches. The road was thick ice. We had to drive about five or ten miles an hour. When we got near Pontiac or Chenoa or one of those towns, we heard a report on the local radio that if your electricity was still off, you could go to this school; they were offering food there, chili and hot dogs.

We had just made a turn in that direction and were driving through this town when we happened to notice this fellow coming out of the driveway of a motel. Instead, we made a quick turn into the motel. The guy had just checked out and we grabbed the room. The three of us entered that room and all just collapsed on this one double bed. We were lying sideways on the bed and immediately we all fell asleep. We stayed like that until the next morning.

The next day we got back on the road and made it to downtown Chicago. When we got near the Rock Island Station I dropped off Ev and Jack and then returned the car to Hertz. Of course, the car was all banged up. The Hertz guy was looking at the car, and I figured I'd better start talking, so I started going on about how those people in Indianapolis should have told us there was snow up here in Chicago. How I couldn't imagine why they had rented us this car. Why anyone would even think of letting us take this car out in this kind of weather! How of course we got stuck and had to get towed.

The Hertz representative listened to all this. "Oh, don't worry," he said. "We're awfully sorry, blah, blah." And that was that. I turned in the car, jumped on the train and got home about noon. My wife was out shoveling snow. Everybody was out shoveling snow, all the kids and neighbors. Naturally, throughout all this we couldn't call home. All the lines had been down. So for a couple of days no one knew where the heck I was.

Obviously, it was sheer stupidity that we got caught in this, even though we said we're not stupid. But stupid is as stupid does.

RAYMOND EPICH

Anything to Get Out of Toledo

All consultants will identify with this. You're in a small town where there are very few flights out. If you miss the last plane, you either stay over or start driving to the next big town. We had a large client in Toledo we were visiting on one occasion. As usual, the meetings ran late and we were speeding out I-90 to the airport for the last plane. We ran right by the exit for the airport and were headed west toward Fort Wayne. So I said to my partner who was staying behind at the client site, "Do a U-turn across the median and go back to the eastbound exit."

It was a toll road and he said, "I can't, I have a ticket showing me heading west."

I said, "Throw the damn ticket away. We'll tell them we inadvertently left it in a roadside restaurant on the way over here."

"Gosh, that will cost us seven dollars." he said. He was always tight with money.

I had to agree to pay the seven dollars and the cost of a ticket if the police caught us doing the U-turn. Well, we finally we made it to the airport, and on time for the plane home.

RICHARD METZLER

Is Delaware On the Way to Philadelphia?

I was flying out of O'Hare in the winter of '95 with a colleague who lived in the Philadelphia area. We thought, let's just get to the East Coast. Part of the travel game is that you just try and get as close to your destination as possible.

So, we had to catch a 6:00 p.m. flight to Philadelphia. But the 6:00 p.m. flight became a 7:00 p.m. flight, then a 9:00 p.m. flight, and then I think we ended up leaving around midnight, on a flight to Newark, which was as close as we could get. We figured we could rent a car or catch a taxi from Newark, which is about an hour and a half from Philadelphia.

By the time we got to Newark, there were no rental cars and no taxis to take us to Philadelphia, only a bunch of these guys who stand around saying, "Need a ride, need a ride." We asked this one fellow how much it would cost to take us to Philadelphia. He said, 300 bucks! We negotiated him down to $220 and climbed in his car. But you have to picture this. We're in something like a '72 Ford Thunderbird. It's an old, beat-up car and the driver has this one long front seat that's pushed all the way back, which gave us about 12 inches of leg room in the back.

The guy wasn't leaving Newark until we paid him, either, so we ended up driving around Newark for half an hour looking for a cash machine. Finally, we got our money and paid him and we were off. Or so we thought. Then the guy told us he didn't know how to get to Philadelphia. You know, there is actually only one highway between Newark and Philadelphia. You can't miss it. You get on the highway and you don't stop until you get to Philadelphia. It's not that hard. It wasn't a good sign.

I was tired and just wanted to sleep, so I told my colleague, you deal with this guy. So the two of them chatted while I pretended to sleep. After a while I guess we both dozed off. The next thing we knew, the driver was asking us, is Delaware on the way to Philadelphia? You can be sure that woke us up! This guy had overshot Pennsylvania and we were now an hour past Philadelphia. We were on our way to Washington, D.C., two and a half hours into what should have been an hour and a half drive. And we were still an hour-and-a-half from Philadelphia! It was a long night.

STEVE GOLDFIELD

You Can't Get There from Here

The problems you can't anticipate are the client-driven, short-term schedule changes. This story is a winter adventure. I was in Seattle trying to get to Los Angeles. It turned out I had to come back to visit a client in New York, so I flew from Seattle back to New York on a Wednesday night. I worked with the client on Thursday and attended a board meeting on Friday afternoon. I had nailed down my travel arrangements to fly out at six o'clock Friday evening back to Los Angeles. There was a major evening event on Saturday I was supposed to attend.

However, because it was a President's Day weekend school break, I couldn't get anything nonstop. I then booked a Delta flight through Salt Lake City, connecting to Los Angeles. When I got out to JFK, I could see that the weather was not good. It was warm and foggy and the inbound planes weren't able to come in. I actually got to the airport early, which was rare for me, so I went to the Crown Room to check in. The woman at the desk said, "Hello, sir, this is going to be a gate check-in. You'll have to get your seat at the gate." Of course, I asked the next question, which was does this mean the flight's oversold. She was being basically being non-communicative, and I knew what that meant. The flight was oversold.

Well, I went out to the gate and stood in line for 45 minutes. Finally, I got up to the counter and presented my ticket. I was told I would have to wait to get my seat assignment until later. I knew I was either going to get bumped or something bad was going to happen. The plane itself hadn't even landed yet. So back I went to the Crown Room; I wanted to see if I could find another flight going west. By then the agent was confessing that they were oversold. Typically, they oversell by about 10 percent. This flight was oversold by 18 seats. Plus, there were rug rats all over the place, it being a school holiday.

Now, remember, this was before Frequent Flyer Clubs, so I wasn't exactly in a position to pull rank or anything. So there I was, booked on a plane that was not on the ground yet, and I had to connect through Salt Lake City. They were saying it might be another hour before it would arrive. Of course, then they would have to get the people off the plane. Well, I made a simple calculation: I was not going to make my connection. I decided to go home.

On the way home I called this super special American Express travel expert on the emergency line. I'd kind of given up but I just wanted to see if there were any other options. Nothing! Well, what did they have going to Chicago? Nothing! Okay, how about White Plains? Yes, they did have a 6:50 a.m. flight from White Plains to Chicago. But from Chicago west there was absolutely nothing, except weather problems and a lot of cancelled flights. I told them just get me to Chicago and I would take my chances.

The American Express person came up with this scenario. If I flew to Chicago, I could make an illegal connect on a Delta flight back to Cincinnati, then go from Cincinnati to Los Angeles. An illegal connect *used* to be any connection with 30 minutes or less between flights from different terminals. In O'Hare, if you're changing terminals they wanted an hour between landing and departure. Maybe you can get 45 minutes. But 30 minutes or less was definitely illegal.

I said, okay, just do it as separate legs with separate tickets. That way the airlines wouldn't know what I was doing. You have to keep in mind that I was arranging all this while in the back of a limo going back to Connecticut. I didn't have my own air guide out. So the next morning when I got to White Plains, lo and behold what was taking off at six o'clock but a Delta flight to Cincinnati. That meant I could have flown straight to Cincinnati out of White Plains, instead of going to Chicago first. And that flight had empty seats, too, because I went and checked.

Instead, I had to get on the United flight to Chicago. That flight turned out to be an hour late, and I ended up missing my connection. It was by then about nine-thirty in the morning Chicago time, and I was at the end of the C Concourse, checking the departure board, looking for any flight scheduled to go anyplace on the West Coast. San Diego, Orange County, or Los Angeles, I didn't care. It turned out there were three flights all cued up to leave. Naturally, they were all at the other end of the terminal. So I had to race all the way to the other end of O'Hare.

I decided to go for the Los Angeles flight. Forget it. It was overbooked and departing late because of problems. Then I went for the San Diego flight. Same story. I ran over to the Orange County flight. It was already 10 minutes past departure but everyone was still milling around. I walked up

"Are we there yet?"

and asked if I could get on this flight. The agent said all they had left was four first-class seats. Yes, great! I'll take one. Well no, the agent said, I couldn't have one because they had people who had already requested upgrades. Okay, how about if they gave me one of the seats those people were vacating? Bingo. She upgraded somebody else, gave me a seat, and in five minutes I was on the plane. I ended up landing at Orange County at twelve-thirty. I rented a car, drove to Los Angeles, and was where I wanted to be by two-thirty in the afternoon.

ANONYMOUS A

OCCASIONALLY IT JUST GETS TO YOU

I'm Going to Have You Shot!

I took some time off from consulting to work for United Airlines. While at work, I used to hear these stories of people who had worked at ticket counters or who had worked at airports, and all I could think was that these poor people behind the counter have absolutely the worst job in the world.

One of the stories I heard was from a guy who worked at the Boston terminal. They had refused boarding to a woman who was obviously drunk. Her excuse apparently was that the only way she could fly was if she was out of it. But they weren't going to let her on because of her condition.

Now, this was a fairly good-sized woman. So she backed up to get a running start and then just barreled straight toward the entry. My friend was standing in the doorway. He was a pretty good-sized guy too. He quickly grabbed two others and they locked arms. This woman came running at them and tried to bowl them over. Fortunately, they held their ground. The woman stepped back. She looked at my friend. "My son is a Boston policeman," she screamed. "I'm going to have him shoot you!" Then she turned around and stormed away.

I've heard all sorts of stories like these; they just go on and on. It's unbelievable what people will do.

ROBERT ARNOLD

I'm Getting a Little Past Sanity Here!

This is the story of the trip from hell. Our firm at the time was a small firm that did two things. We did compensation consulting, and we did bank officer salary surveys. We had 1,400 to1,500 banks around the country participating in this survey, and we had to go out and visit all of them every two or three years to make sure the data was correct and that they felt good about the survey and how to use it. So young consultants like me would make these trips around the country, visiting all these banks.

I had a compensation consulting client, a bank in Blue Island, Illinois, that I had to meet with on a Friday. I was supposed to deliver this big report to them. There were no faxes back then, no Federal Express, and if you went through the Post Office it could take a very long time, so we personally delivered reports. Since the meeting was on a Friday, I had Monday through Thursday to visit all the banks in the area. It was four banks a day in some places—in Wisconsin, I went to three or four cities in one day, hopping around in puddle jumpers.

So I left on that Monday and I arrived at O'Hare, which I passed through about six times during this damn trip. I got to O'Hare and my bag was lost, but the airline people assured that they would deliver it to the hotel that night. But the bag didn't show up. So now I was traveling around with my briefcase and the suit and shirt and tie I had on. The airline was so sure my bag would be there by Tuesday that I thought it would be kind of silly to go out and buy any more clothes. But by the night of the second day, I went out and bought some clothes—another shirt and a set of underwear. The baggage still didn't show up.

Of course, the reason I was really worried about the bag was that the report I was going to deliver on Friday was in it. The only way I could have a useful meeting was to use a lot of compensation data and things that were in the report. Without the report, I would have had to have a photographic memory to make this meeting work. I needed that report. And by Wednesday it still hadn't come.

Thursday was the worst day of this trip. Funny and different and bad things had happened Tuesday and Wednesday, but Thursday was the absolute worst. After seeing four banks in three towns, I was to get the last flight from Peoria to Chicago around 6:30 at night. Well, the flight was delayed and then canceled. They brought out the ricketiest old bus I'd ever seen and said, "Don't worry, we'll drive you all to O'Hare." I didn't want to drive in a big, stupid bus with a lot of angry people to O'Hare, so I went to Avis and asked for the best car they had to rent. I put the pedal to the metal and I went as fast as I could up to O'Hare. I drove to O'Hare right past Blue Island, Illinois, because I was assured my bags (and my report) were at O'Hare.

I got to O'Hare, parked in the public parking lot, and went to American's luggage area. They didn't have my bag, but they thought it might be down at Delta. I had to go from one end of the old O'Hare terminal to the other end to find that no, my bag wasn't there either. In fact, Delta thought it was back with American, but when they called American they hadn't been able to find it. They promised me they'd try to deliver it to my hotel if it showed up. But by now I figured it was irretrievably lost.

I realized I'd have to figure out how to deal with this client at nine o'-clock tomorrow morning. It was now one in the morning. I went out to get my car, and found that some prankster or thug had slashed all four tires! They were all down to the rims. I had reached the point where you couldn't make me angry any more, so many bad things had happened. I'd gone over the edge, and so with a big smile on my face, carrying my briefcase and a little shopping bag with my dirty laundry in it, I walked up to the Avis counter.

"You've got a real problem with your car out in the public parking lot," I said, "and I need another one." I explained what had happened, and soon I had another car. I drove back down to Blue Island, Illinois, arriving there at about two in the morning. By the time I got there, I was completely exhausted and had no idea what I was going to do the next morning.

Then I went to check in and gave the guy at the counter my confirmation number. He looked at me kind of nervously, and said they didn't have any rooms left. I said, "Oh jeez, you know you can't find a room this time of night. You've got to have a room left!"

He said no, they didn't, so I yelled at him a little bit. And he said, "Well, actually we do have one room but I was told it was a late arrival and that I should hold it no matter how late it is."

I said, "Well, no matter how late it is, I am here." And I grabbed him by the collar and I said, "You won't believe the trip I've had, and I'm getting a little past sanity here!" So the guy agreed to give me the room. He was a little nervous, so he just turned around and grabbed a key.

I walked down to the room and threw open the door. Guess what? The room was not empty. There was a couple there, a man and a woman on the bed with a little light on, and they were not asleep. Let's just say they weren't watching TV.

I realized a terrible mistake had been made here. "I'm very sorry. He gave me the wrong key," and I closed the door. Apparently, neither of them had heart attacks, but I did hear some loud conversation going on in the room. So I walked back down the hall to the front desk, where the guy apologized and gave me the right key. I slept until about eight o'clock, got up, and got myself into as good shape as I possibly could. As I drove over to the bank, I was so tired I ended up backing right into a brick wall. It did major damage to the rear end of the car, but I could still drive it. When I finally met with the client, I told him the story and why I didn't have the report. He didn't laugh much and was a little unhappy, but I apologized and came back two weeks later.

PETE SMITH

Where the Hell Am I?

All consultants occasionally get the schedule where you have to be in five or six different cities in a week. Up early in the morning, quick shower and shave, coffee and donut and off to a meeting with a client; then a behind schedule, too fast taxi ride to the airport to barely catch your plane to the next city. Usually, there is a team on site and you have dinner, some wine, and stay up too late.

One week I was on the west coast. I started in Chicago on Sunday night to San Francisco, Monday to Seattle, Tuesday to Los Angeles, Wednesday to Spokane, and Thursday night back to San Francisco.

The alarm goes off at 6 a.m, and I look around the hotel room, and I honestly can't remember where I am. I'm totally confused. And I can't find my glasses to read the match cover on the bedside table. Finally, I open the window shade and see heavy fog. By process of elimination, I narrow down the possibilities to either London or San Francisco. I actually called the front desk to find out where the hell I was.

RICHARD METZLER

THE RULES TO SURVIVE ALL OF THIS

Zen for the Road

It's not that I would ever say that traveling is a good thing. But you sure do grow from it. Everybody changes dramatically for the better from travel. Travel is basically training for crisis handling. I was probably on the road 10 years before I reached the point that no matter what happened, I calmly accepted it. What if your flight is delayed and you can't get home? How do you deal with that? A very new consultant deals with it quite differently than a more experienced one. The more experienced one knows all the tricks. They calmly go about circumventing the regular system. While the rest of the population gets in line to wait to talk to an agent about rerouting, the experienced consultant knows to open their cell phone, call the travel agent, and get rerouted from there. He or she becomes very competent and that competence breeds confidence. That confidence can then spill over into everything he or she does, too.

It's the Zen approach to travel, I guess. You learn to accept that it's going to work out and if you don't get home that night, that's okay. You learn that getting upset is not going to make things work any better.

CYNTHIA DRISKILL

Damage, What Damage?

The rule about rental cars is whatever condition you return it in is the condition it was in when you took it. I mean, things happen. You left the car in the valet park. Who knows what happened? Ignorance is the absolute imperative in this deal. I had a situation once where I was sitting in a lot of traffic at a railroad crossing. It was a slow freight train and I'm 20 cars back. It looked like a 20 minute delay. It also looked like I was going to be late for my flight.

But I also knew a way around. I could make a U-turn and go back the other way. So I turned the wheel as far as I could to go left so I'd miss the car in front of me. Now, think about the two lanes coming the other way. There's no traffic because of the train, right? You'd think all I had to worry about was the car in front of me. So as soon as I cleared the car in front, I kind of half-floored it to make my U-turn. What did I do? I pulled right out into the path of a semi coming the wrong way. He was about to turn into a warehouse terminal that was just before the railroad tracks. Of course, the truck hit me in the left front fender. The bumper was history.

Well, I jumped out. He jumped out. It didn't look like I could drive the car. I told the guy I was late for a plane and he went back to his cab and got a crowbar and pulled the fender away from the tire. Great! Now at least I could drive. I took off and dropped the car off at the wrong return place. Three weeks later I got a letter saying the car was damaged. What could have happened? I wrote back and said, well, it didn't drive very well and there were some strange noises, but as far as the missing bumper goes, I just had no idea. It was a mystery.

ANONYMOUS A

Rules for the Road—Pocket Version

For most consultants the worst stories take place when they have to travel with their spouse. A lot of things can happen. First, you lose a lot of flexibility. Even if you carry your luggage on, you're not going to move as fast as you normally would. And if finding one seat is difficult, finding two seats is even harder. If your spouse doesn't travel a lot, she's also going to look at you and say things like, "How can they do that to you? Why don't you go yell at 'em?" It doesn't help.

Some hotels are also challenging. You have a guaranteed late arrival. You show up. It's midnight. The plane was late and they've sold your room. What do you do now? In this case, you push as hard as you can because they were supposed to hold your room. You had a quote with a guaranteed late arrival. One of the things you always do is keep your reservation numbers written in your diary. What's your confirmation number? If they've sold you out and recommend that you go over to the last chance motel, you basically do everything you can to force them to give you another room. They can sell somebody else out of a room. Typically, that's the game. There's almost never a case when a room is not available.

Basically you just can't let anything upset you. Just observe the rules, keep on moving. Okay, that won't work. What about this? What about that?

Also, never get angry with an agent. They're stuck with the problem. They didn't cause it. And try not to go places that you know are trouble. Like don't ever go to Detroit. I mean, if you can keep from going to Detroit, do it. That way you can avoid flying Northwest.

ANONYMOUS A

Only On Weekends

Consulting is an all consuming profession, particularly if you're a partner and trying to build a business. I always felt that one of the keys to success in the market was being with your clients. I was there in the morning ready with the coffee when they came, and I was there at night after they left to turn out the lights and put out the cat.

But being with a client means not being home with your family. After a few years of friction over this point, my wife, my kids and I came to an agreement: All birthdays and anniversaries were to be celebrated on weekends. Other special days like graduations and holidays were celebrated on schedule of course. But our kids never had a birthday on a weekday. This wasn't a perfect solution but it worked for us.

RICHARD METZLER

Never Check a Bag

I did learn very early in my career never to check a bag. I was presenting to a board of directors in Muscatine, Iowa, and flew in a pair of cut-off's and T-shirt with a pair of sandals. I had a stopover at the O'Hare Hilton before my flight the next morning. Well, my bag didn't arrive until about three in the morning. It was a close call. The CEO at this firm reminded me of the farmer in that old Grant Wood painting, kind of stern and puritan. I can imagine what he would have thought seeing me show up in shorts and a T-shirt. Actually, he was a great guy. He probably would have gotten quite a laugh out of it.

ALAN ANDOLSEN

That's Your Air, This is My Air

I have to tell you this frequent flyer tip that I learned from my son. It does not work on all planes, obviously, but it does work on a 737, which we often fly on. The thing I hate the most when flying, and the thing that most people hate, is when the fellow in front of you leans his seat back into your lap. Normally, if you're a frequent flyer you board earlier. So my son taught me that as soon as you get on a plane, you take all the air vents in a row, point them toward the seat in front of you, and turn them on. Then when the person arrives and sits in his seat, if he leans his seat back even five degrees he'll have the air blowing right on his head. Immediately, he'll turn around and say, "Your air is blowing on my head." And you say, "Yes, that's my air. Your air is in front of you. That little thing there will adjust your air, but this is my air. And this is where it's going to stay." Believe me, there's no leaning back after that. Now, that only works on planes where you can adjust it to the correct angle. On the wide-bodies you can't adjust the air. But it's a good trick. Not too many people know this one.

RAYMOND EPICH

Take a Deep Breath and Treat Yourself Well

My technique for handling travel is deep breathing. I try to close my eyes and just sort of let it happen, just breathe. Breathe very deeply. That's about the only way I can get through the panic. Another thing I've also learned over the years about being on the road is to treat yourself well. I'm not talking about eating big meals or things like that. In my case, I'm an art and music lover so I'll take some time for myself and go to a museum or a concert. Do something like that. Instead of always pushing 16 hours a day, I push 12 and take four hours for myself. That's what works for me. I'm much stronger then. Of course, it took me eight or nine years to learn these things.

If I'm abroad, I'll try to make it a weekend and take Saturday and Sunday to get to know the area or do something fun, rather than just flying in there, doing business and then running out. I know other major firms are more restrictive on travel policy. But with the flexibility we have at our firm, I can do that. So I think I've learned to pace myself a little better. No less productively, but just making sure I spend some time for myself.

ALAN ANDOLSEN

One Iron-Clad Rule

I think it's very difficult to have dual careers and maintain a marriage. It's very demanding. In terms of travel and relationships, are there any secrets? An absolute iron-clad rule that my husband and I have, because we both travel a lot in our jobs right now, is to communicate often and completely. A technique that is useful is to give each other complete contact and schedule information. Maybe once every two weeks we synchronize our calendars. We do this even though we don't have children at home anymore. We try as much as possible to coordinate our travel, to schedule our trips at the same time. That way we're away from home for the smallest chunk of time, and at the same time.

ELIZABETH KOVACS

A Briefcase to Do Surgery

I was traveling with a senior partner from Los Angeles to Philadelphia with my bag checked through to New York. This was in January in the middle of winter. My plan was to have some flight time with him and then pick up a shuttle to New York. So all I had with me was a light raincoat, which I had packed in my bag and checked.

Well, the flight was more than two hours late taking off. Then when we finally took off one of the hydraulic lines burst causing an engine to burst into flames. So we doubled back to Los Angeles. While waiting for the plane to be repaired, I found out there was a flight directly to JFK with another airline two gates over. They said they would transfer my bag, so I took that flight. I got the last seat on the plane and arrived at JFK at four in the morning.

Unfortunately, my bag obviously hadn't made the transfer. So there I was unshaven with no coat and at the wrong terminal. It's four in the morning in the middle of winter and I had to get around to the other terminal for my car. I got to the car only to discover the battery was dead. I ended up banging on the door to get one of the maintenance people to let me back into the locked terminal. I called a tow truck, and while I was waiting I bought a travel kit to shave. Believe it or not, I had an interview scheduled in a couple of hours at the office with a prospective employee. I don't think I arrived home until about 3 p.m. that Saturday afternoon.

I lost my bag on another occasion, too, on my first trip to Indonesia. I was bringing back all these souvenirs and the airline lost my bag; it ended up in Karachi or somewhere. I got it back to New York City; put it on a van, and had delivered it to the Exxon building. Well, a block from the Exxon building they made another delivery, and while they were stopped, my suitcase was stolen from the back of the van!

The thing you keep in mind through it all is to stay calm. Getting excited isn't going to do you any good anyway. I've also learned over the years to keep my briefcase with me at all times. I keep enough in there that it looks like I can do open heart surgery. I carry razors, bandages and enough essentials to survive for two days. If I can help it, I never check my bag. I also never run for planes and I carry lots of reading material, because you know you're going to have a certain percentage of late flights.

Those are my basic rules for survival. It all comes down to staying relaxed. It helps to pack some Tylenol, too.

EDWARD PRINGLE

BUT IT'S NOT ALL BAD

I Invented the Frequent Flyer Idea

I keep a running total of how many miles I've flown. I'm up to something like 2,400,000. My goal is to get the two and a half million, more or less for a career total. I got a million mile plaque from United way back in 1968. Then American gave me some sort of city destination plaques. But just think of all the prizes we could have gotten in those early days if they had frequent flyer programs.

Actually, I think I invented the frequent flyer idea. There was a guy named Ziegler from American Airlines who was their marketing VP. They had mailed a questionnaire to me, asking if I could think of any ideas to increase their market share. I said, why don't you have something like Green Stamps where you can accumulate points as you fly? Then you'd be predisposed to fly with a certain airline. Next thing I knew along came a frequent flyer program, but there was no prize for old Ray. Nothing! I'm sure it was the equivalent idea. You just don't have to lick the stamps.

RAYMOND EPICH

You Don't Have to Talk

In the early days when I was at home we were eating a lot of leftovers. But when you're on the road, you're sleeping on fresh, ironed sheets. Eating exactly what you want to eat. And you don't have to talk. As a consultant, you talk and listen all day. Then you go home and what do you have to do? You've got to listen and talk some more or you're not doing your job. Sometimes it can be kind of nice to just tune out and watch the Knicks.

MIKE LAPORTA

You Must Be Mr. Smith

I had a client in Crossette, Arkansas, where I had never been. Another client of mine referred the client to me, and he decided to hire me based on the referral, without meeting me. So I scheduled a time to go at the end of a fairly busy travel week, on a Wednesday or Thursday. I got into Crossette—a nice little town—and went into the Crossette Arms Hotel, which they told me was the only place to stay in town. It was summertime, a very hot summer day in late June.

I walked into the hotel at about six p.m. with my two bags. The desk clerk looked up and said, "You must be Mr. Smith." I said, "That's really good, how did you do that?" "The other two have checked in already."

I explained that I had a long trip, and asked where was the best place to eat. I wanted great Southern food. He said, "You're in luck. It's right here. It's the only restaurant in town and it's open until 6:30 p.m.. So if you wash up real quick and get down there I'm sure they'll serve you."

So I went down to the restaurant, sat down, and asked for a double Beefeater martini. She said, "Oh, sir, this is a dry town." I said, "Oh, of course, Arkansas, that's right. Would you give me a beer, a glass of wine – either one would be fine." "This is a dry town. You have to bring in your own beer." I said, "Well, let's see, you're closing in 20 minutes . . . how far is the liquor store?" She said it was 35 miles away because this was a dry county. But that was okay. I had southern fried chicken with milk and it was really good.

Now, I didn't happen to have a book with me on this trip, and I was in this place with nothing going on, nothing to do. I went to my room and the TV didn't work, it's all snow. I remembered seeing a movie theater right across the street as I drove in, so I walked out and sure enough there was a big marquee that said, "Closed for the season." So that was out.

I didn't want to go to sleep at 6:30 or seven in the evening, so I decided to take a little walk. As I walked, I heard some noise that sounded like cheering about three blocks away. I followed the cheering for a bit. It turns out to be a baseball field—middle America at its best. It was the Babe Ruth league finals or something like that. Crossette was playing El Dorado, its biggest rival. The stands were filled with people in this nice little park. It was the second inning, the sun was beginning to set, there were beautiful colors all around, and the lights were on in the stadium. So I watched for about an inning or so. It was great to watch these kids; I was just sitting there relaxing with my shirt sleeves rolled up and my tie down. It was something to do.

All of the sudden there was a hand on my shoulder and a voice said, "You must be Mr. Smith." What a great town, right? I turned around and said, "I am, who are you?"

He was the fellow I was going to be working with. He said, you're the consultant that I've never met that I'm going to be working with. You're the only person I know of who would be in town tonight with a tie on."

We ended up watching the game, going out to his houseboat for drinks afterwards, and having dinner at his home the next night. As badly as it started, it was one of the best trips I ever had. I guess the moral of the story is that sometimes traveling can be fun.

PETE SMITH

Stirred, Not Shaken

Travel is not as much fun as it used to be. I remember an occasion soon after I joined McKinsey when I had a black tie event in New York to attend. Then I had to immediately fly out to San Francisco to meet with Tom Peters. I was traveling first class on Pan Am out of Kennedy, which in those days was not so egregiously priced. It turned out I was one of only two people in first class. I was a bachelor then so there I was in my tuxedo, drinking champagne, all the way to San Francisco. I'd like to think it was an elegant sight. You know, if somebody had said, what's your name, I could have said "Bond, James Bond."

Today, the planes are more like cow cars and the airport restaurants are crowded. You're also just tired. In the old days, the 747s had a bar and lounge upstairs. This wasn't so-called business class. It used to be if I went to a meeting in Madrid, I'd stay around for a couple of extra days. We'd do our work and develop all sorts of new ideas. Everybody was having fun. Friday would roll around and nobody would want to go home. Instead, you'd rent a car and go to the Escoril or to the major museums. If you were in Stockholm on Midsummer Nights eve, as I was, you'd hit the discos, admire all the gorgeous Scandinavian women, watch the midnight sun go down and come back up again five minutes later. All the while saying to yourself, I'm getting paid for this. But all that's history now.

BILL MATASSONI

Steak and an Invoice

On a project in Akron, Ohio, I once went to a local restaurant and ate a nice steak dinner. When I was done, I asked for the check and then put my American Express card down.

"Sorry, we don't take those," said the waitress. Okay. I reached in my wallet and got out the MasterCard and put that down. "Sir, I said we don't take those." "Well, this is a different credit card." "I mean, we don't take credit cards."

"Well, this could be a problem. I don't have much cash on me."

"It's not a problem. Just give me your business card. We'll send you an invoice."

Sure enough the next week the invoice came. That was their normal way of doing business. They opted just to bill people and save the credit card expense. This was a high-priced restaurant near the business center in downtown Akron. But definitely of the old school.

COBY FRAMPTON

And the Way It Should Always Be

A former golf partner of mine had retired and moved to Hilton Head. It was springtime and I said to myself, I've got to get out and play some golf. So I decided to go down to Hilton Head on a Thursday evening, and my wife would follow on Friday.

On Thursday evening, I walked into O'Hare. I was using frequent flyer miles, mind you, so there was no revenue for American Airlines on this trip. I'd been flying back and forth to Houston on a consulting job for about 18 months, so at that point I was platinum executive, or whatever the highest rank is. The flight was supposed take me to Raleigh-Durham, and then on to Hilton Head with a one hour connection between flights. But there was a mechanical problem at O'Hare and a one-hour delay. When we finally pulled away from the gate, the captain came on to tell us he thought he could make up some of the time. I'm thinking, yeah, right. But somehow we did manage to land in Raleigh-Durham within a few minutes of my connecting flight's departure.

The Raleigh-Durham airport has a real long concourse, and we pulled in at one end. The connection was an American Eagle flight, and of course, they were operating out of the other end of this long concourse. So we landed and pulled up to the gate. The gate agent came on and said, welcome to Raleigh-Durham, unfortunately all the connecting flights have to leave and we apologize, blah, blah, blah. Of course, there was a lot of grumbling. I was trying to get out and everybody was standing in the aisle. I was standing there waiting, and it took several minutes as everyone slowly moved off the airplane.

Then I heard an announcement. "Will passenger Arnold please identify himself to the gate agent?" I was thinking, "Oh, great, now they're going to give me a hotel room." My friend and I had an 8:00 o'clock tee time the next morning. I didn't want a hotel room. Well, I walked out to the gate agent and identified myself. He just said, okay, let's go. There was a cart sitting right there, and he grabbed me by the arm, plopped me in the cart and we drove the length of the concourse. I was wondering what in the world was going on?

We got to the American Eagle end of the concourse and there was absolutely nobody in sight. By then I was thinking, "You turkey, you brought me all the way down here, got my hopes up and now nothing's going to come of it." But then he said, "See that door over there? Go out that door and you'll see a van at the bottom of the stairs. He'll take you to your flight." Wow! And I hadn't complained or bitched to anybody. What was this about?

I walked down the stairs and sure enough there was an empty van sitting there with a driver. I walked up to the van and the driver looked at me. "Are you Mr. Arnold?" "Well, yes I am." "Okay, let's go." And we raced across the tarmac past all these American Eagle planes all buttoned up for the night. There was only one plane out there with the lights on. As we got closer, I could see that the stairs in the rear were still down. It was one of those small American Eagle planes where you board from the rear. We pulled up and there was a stewardess standing there.

"Mr. Arnold, we are so glad you made it," she said, "we've been waiting for you." They had delayed the flight 20 minutes just for me! Of course, I couldn't let well enough alone. About halfway up the stairs I had the brass to ask, "Uh, by the way, is there any chance my luggage, in particular my golf clubs, can make it?" She said, "I'm sorry, but we can't wait any longer. And by the way, there's only one seat left and it's up in the front compartment."

I was thinking, "Oh man, all of these people have been sitting there, they're going watch me walk up the aisle and just shoot daggers at me. They're going to wonder, who is this SOB? And why am I sitting here waiting for him?" Somehow I made it up to my seat, sat down and buckled up. I was looking for something to read when all of a sudden, the attendant appeared over my shoulder and whispered very quietly, "Your golf clubs will be here in just a minute."

Honest to God, as I sat there, I heard two thumps. There were my bag and my golf clubs being loaded on. Then they closed the luggage compartment, started up the engines, and we took off. I thought to myself, isn't that something? The only thing I could come up with is that because of my status, they had decided to be nice and take care of me. I've certainly never heard another story like that.

ROBERT ARNOLD

PLANES, TRAINS, HOTELS, AND RENTAL CARS
(AND OTHER GOOD STORIES)

A One-Man Show

One time I was scheduled on a commuter flight from a small upstate New York town to New York City. I was flying out of a small airport in the middle of winter. I arrived at the check-in and a man came out and took the ticket. He looked it over and then gave me my boarding pass. He told me we'd go through security shortly. A few minutes later we were called over to go through the metal detector. The same guy was now supervising the walk-through. Later, I walked outside with my bag. This guy was now out there, loading the bags on the plane!

Well, you can guess where this is going. I got on the plane and this fellow was now on the speaker informing us that he would be our pilot for the flight. He announced that once we'd taken off and climbed to altitude, should we happen to need anything, to just ring the call button. He'd be glad to put the plane on autopilot and see what we needed.

To make matters worse on this one-man show, the flight to LaGuardia was very cold and bumpy. And on our approach we got stuck in a long holding pattern. Everyone had his or her big overcoats and gloves on, scarves and hats. At one point it got so rough I thought a little fresh air might be appropriate. I didn't want to get airsick. I had pulled my glove off and reached up to open the air vent. Well, it was like grabbing an ice tray out of the freezer, it was so cold. My fingers just stuck to it. I felt like the little boy who on a dare stuck his tongue to a flagpole.

I thought to myself, look at the situation I'm in. My hand is stuck to the overhead vent, and I'm flying on a plane with a pilot who will gladly put the aircraft on autopilot to get us a drink or something. Travel can certainly be interesting at times.

COBY FRAMPTON

To Get to the Head of the Line

I was on a flight out of O'Hare to LaGuardia that was delayed because of weather. We just sat out there on the tarmac. It ended up being a four or four-and-a-half hour flight. The guy next to me never did anything except sit there and stare out the window. You could see by his expression that he was ticked. He just sat there for four and a half hours like that.

Toward the end of this flight as we were coming in for the approach, a woman came from the back of the airplane—I was sitting at the bulkhead— she walked all the way up to go to the lavatory in the first class cabin. The lights were on and we're supposed to have our seat belts fastened. I can see the flight attendants trying to figure out what to do. Finally, they make an announcement, "Everybody must return to their seats, we're now on our final approach." Nothing happens. A flight attendant then got up and knocked on the door, asking the woman to please hurry. Again, nothing. By now we've banked around and we're coming in for the landing. Now the attendant knocks on the door and tells the woman to just hold on and stay where you are.

Well, we land and guess what? The woman opens the door and walks out, the first one off the airplane. She just wanted to get to the head of the line. And all I could conclude was, well, that's a New Yorker for you.

ROBERT ARNOLD

Here, Let Me Help

I was flying from Chicago to Saint Louis on the early morning Delta flight. It's only an hour and they used to squeeze in breakfast. I was sitting on the aisle and next to me was a very attractive younger lady going to Saint Louis for a job interview. She was wearing a well-tailored suit with just the correct amount of attractive décolletage showing.

All airlines serve orange juice in little plastic containers with a sealed aluminum top that is very hard to get off. She was struggling with this container and I said, "There's a trick to doing that. You break the vacuum by poking through the top with a sharp object—usually a pencil is handy."

To demonstrate, I pull out a pencil from my shirt pocket and poke the top of her orange juice container. She must have pulled it partly off because when I hit the top of her juice, it squirted right onto her attractive décolletage. The juice ran down the inside of her well-tailored suit and she shivered.

She turned slowly, looked me right in the eye, and said, "You son of a bitch."

We landed without further conversation.

RICHARD METZLER

No, I Never Did Pay

We had a project where we were going from public utility commission to public utility commission giving updates. We had an update scheduled with the officer in charge of a major southern utility. Characteristically, he wanted to meet with us at 8 a.m. on the Tuesday morning after Labor Day. We're based in Chicago while he's way below the Mason-Dixon Line, in a place without many flights. To be there by early Tuesday morning, we would have to leave Chicago on Labor Day. You can imagine how happy we were about that.

On Labor Day, we were on the plane. But there was some kind of delay and we were just waiting and waiting. Finally, we took off and it seemed like it took 45 minutes just to get over Lake Michigan. It was just taking forever to get going. Then we took a left along the lakeshore and the plane started dumping fuel over the lake. This was up toward the northern suburbs. Then the plane turned around and it was apparent that we were coming back in to land. Eventually the captain came on to report that we had a problem and had to land. As we were coming in I could see a whole line of emergency equipment on the runway waiting for us. The flight attendant ordered us to get into the tuck position. Obviously, we did as we were told.

Fortunately, everything turned out okay and we landed safely. But we still had to get to our destination and there weren't any other non-stops. We ended up taking a flight that went from Chicago to Dallas to Shreveport, and then we drove on to our client site. We didn't arrive until close to 2:00 in the morning. Apparently, there were only two cabs in this entire city, and there were all these people on the plane. So as soon as the door opened, I ran out and grabbed the first cab. But the first cab driver wouldn't leave until he knew the second cab driver was on his way. So that meant waiting another 20 minutes until the second cab showed up.

Finally, we got to the hotel, which was a Radisson. It was a typical Radisson, all dark wood and faux marble floors. The only thing atypical was that there wasn't a soul around. No signs of life, except for the Muzak, which was blaring. I pounded on the desk. Nothing! I went behind the desk looking. Still nobody! But I did find the key drawer. I opened it and took a key and I just checked myself in. I went up to the room and got a night's sleep. And in the morning I came down, returned the key, thanked the clerk for the room, and just walked away.

No, I never did pay.

JAMES BLOMBERG

We've All Been There (Well, Maybe)

Once, early in my career, I checked into a hotel in a small community. I went to my room, stuck the key in the door and entered, only to find some poor, embarrassed young couple there. Let's just say they were having a wonderful time, and they weren't expecting guests. Of course, I got out of there as quick as I could. The funny thing was I then found myself wondering if someone was going to walk in on me. I ended up propping up a chair in front of my door.

DAVID TIERNO

Be Careful Where You Sit

I have one story that I just love to tell. This was when I was consulting for Coca-Cola in the late '70s. It was one of my earliest jobs. I had just arrived in Atlanta, met with the client, and then went to the hotel in the evening. There was a young woman behind the desk who explained to me that they were right in the middle of renovating the hotel but that she had a really neat room reserved for me.

Great, I thought. So I registered and went on up to the room. I noticed when I stuck the key in the door, the door just opened. It wasn't locked. I thought that was a little weird. But I walked in and it was a really nice room, with a balcony and a platform at one end with a sofa on it. It was a very nice room, except for the two guys standing up on the platform talking. As I walked in with my bags, they very quickly excused themselves and walked out.

Just to make sure, I looked around. Everything seemed okay so I left and went to dinner. I didn't think any more about it. Well, I came back after dinner and sat down on the bed and the entire bed just collapsed on me, all the way to the ground. I mean, the whole thing, the headboard, footboard, mattress and box springs. Bam! All the way down.

My only thought was, Oh shit! But, you know, I was so tired, I just said to myself, I'm just going to sleep on the floor. I'll call in the morning. No big deal. And that's what I did. Morning came and I got up and headed straight to the shower. I was taking my shower when the soap dish fell out of the wall! It was heavy ceramic and just missed my toe. Obviously, they'd not finished gluing the thing in right. Well, so much for the shower. Then I realized there were no towels in the room. Somehow, I managed to dry myself off, dress, and get off to work.

I got back later in the day and saw the clerk at the front desk talking to this wonderful old couple who looked like they were probably on vacation. As I walked by, she asked me what I thought of the room. Without thinking, I just turned around and said, "Well, other than the fact that the bed collapsed, the soap dish fell out of the wall, and there were no towels in the room, it was quite comfortable, thank you." I was kind of distracted and had not really noticed the old couple there. And the look on this young woman's face was just terrible. It was only then that I really noticed the older couple. Standing there with these looks on their faces, like do we really want to stay here? If I had been paying attention, I never would have done that in front of her.

But she did take care of things, and I ended up with a fruit basket for all my trouble.

ALAN ANDOLSEN

'Now, What Exactly Are You Doing In My Car?

I once flew to Minneapolis in the middle of wintertime to see a client. I arrived at the airport and walked over to the Hertz counter to pick up the car.

The woman behind the counter said to me, "You need to know that if the car won't start, we can't come start it for you. But we will pick up the car if you're stranded somewhere." I asked her why she was telling me this. Apparently, a cold front was moving through the area. By next morning it was 26 degrees below zero!

My colleague and I walked out to the parking lot and sure enough the car wouldn't start. Of course, we panicked. We walked back to the terminal and called the client. He said, "Listen, we know how to drive in this climate. I'll have my secretary pick you guys up. She'll be driving a gray Cutlass Sierra and she looks like she's in her late forties or early fifties." That's how he described her. He said she would be there in five or ten minutes.

So we waited just inside the door. All of sudden this gray Cutlass Sierra pulled up, the trunk popped open and a woman got out of the car. I grabbed my bag and charged through the door, threw my bag in the trunk, and jumped in the back seat. My partner did the same thing. Now we're sitting in the back seat of this woman's car.

The woman opened the door. "Who are you?" she says. She didn't look happy. "Well, uh, aren't you from such and such a company?" No, she was not! I really thought she was kidding. She wanted to know what exactly we were doing in her car. Okay, she was not kidding. Big mistake. We apologized and got out.

Five minutes later another gray Cutlass Sierra pulled up, almost identical to the first car. Interesting. The woman in the second car even looked like the first woman.

MICHAEL ALBRECHT

Will the Real Richard Metzler Please Stand Up?

I flew into Albany from Chicago and went to the Hertz Rental counter where I stood in line behind another gentleman, well dressed. My turn comes and I say, "My name is Metzler, I have a reservation."

The Hertz lady says, "Oh, yeah, and my name is Barbara Bush."

Needless to say, I was somewhat taken aback. After several moments of confusion on both of our parts, it turns out that the gentleman in front of me was also named Richard Metzler. What do you suppose the odds are of that"?

We finally got the car contract straightened out and she paged Mr. Metzler to return to the counter. I introduced myself, he was an attorney from Rochester but we couldn't find any connection back through the respective families. We exchanged holiday cards for several years but eventually lost contact.

RICHARD METZLER

Cream Pie Capital of the World

I recall an assignment in a very small Pennsylvania town. I had six young, single guys with me on that engagement. And it was a long, nine-month engagement. The local Denny's was probably the first or second best place to eat, that's how small this town was. We must have eaten there four nights a week. Once or twice a week the motel we stayed at had music and dancing in the dining room. I remember one night someone in our group asked a guy there, "So where's the local hot spot?" The guy just looked at him. "This is it, man."

It's funny when you're on the road the things you remember. Everybody at this place was doing that dance that used to be popular where people would hit their butts together. This was also the first time I ever saw a bunch of women dancing with each other. Apparently, the local wives would hang out at this place. But it's amazing how resourceful people can be in some circumstances. Somehow these young guys managed to make a life out of it. Actually, it got to the point where I had to kind of keep them out of trouble. I guess it didn't hurt that the only place to meet was a bar.

If there is a downside to the smaller towns, there is also from my perspective the opportunity to experience some different corners of American life. That sounds like a cliché, but it's true. In that Pennsylvania town, the fashions were about two years behind everywhere else. Something else I noticed. They had a funny habit of putting cream on every pie they made. I don't think I saw a pie anywhere in town that didn't have cream on it. Apple cream. Blueberry cream. Banana cream. Chocolate cream. I mean they creamed everything! I called this place "the cream pie capital of the world." The small towns definitely have their own uniqueness.

WILLARD ARCHIE

Have You Got a Short One?

All consultants are very aware of the various airline's premium mileage and frequent flyer clubs and their first class upgrade benefits. A number of years ago, the upgrade certificates were paper, and you carried them around to be used when you were able to upgrade from what I call steerage to first class. The upgrades for trips up to 500 miles were called short trips and the ones for longer trips (e.g., over 1000 miles) were called long trips. In the vernacular of the airlines and the frequent travelers, they were called long ones and short ones.

I was in the United Airlines terminal at Newark waiting for the desk agent to clear me for a seat in first class. She called my name in a very loud voice, "Mr. Metzler, please report to the ticket counter." I go over and say, "I'm Mr. Metzler." She says again in a very loud voice, "You're cleared for first class. Do you have a short one?" Everybody in the waiting area heard this, and suddenly everybody stopped talking. In fact, most were chuckling.

Not wanting to miss an opportunity this good, I paused dramatically and say, "Yes, but I make up for it by being very rich." The laughter increased. Not to be outdone, the ticket agent comes right back. "Well alright, you're my kind of man," she says. This brought the house down.

I thought that, Metz, maybe you have a future in standup comedy.

RICHARD METZLER

A Leisurely Morning Drive

We had a client that had its own air force. The CEO of this company was a fanatic about taking off on time. If he said lift off was at six-thirty in the morning, you'd better damn well be on that plane at six-thirty in the morning. If you showed up at six-thirty, that plane was going to be taxiing.

On one occasion, four of us were planning to fly with this CEO and some of his senior people to one of their remote locations, which you couldn't get to by commercial air. Take-off was scheduled for 6:30 the next morning. One of our consultants had a rental car and he was staying at a nearby motel. So the plan was that he would pick up the rest of us. Well, the next morning my phone rang at one minute after five. It was my colleague. Our ride was not there yet. He was supposed to be there at five. What do we do? Okay, where was he staying? We didn't know. All we knew was that he was in some motel. So we both started called every motel in town, and my partner managed to track him down. Woke him up, actually. It was the old story. He didn't get his wake-up call. But by then it didn't matter. The only issue was how quickly could he get in the car and drive.

It was probably a 15-minute trip to get to the other guy's house and then on to my place. The choice we had to make at that point was, do we forget him and take one of our cars? The late sleeper insisted he could be there in ten minutes, so we decided to wait. Well, he was wrong by ten minutes. We didn't leave my house until nearly five-forty, for a trip that is normally a good hour. My partner was behind the wheel and doing everything he could to make time. Meanwhile, the guy who overslept was in the back seat, trying to get dressed.

At one point we came to an intersection with a gas station and just whipped through the station instead of waiting at the red light. Of course, there was a cop sitting right there. Fortunately, our driver was really cool. He jumped out of the car, went back to the policeman, and just started talking. "Look, we were thinking we were going to stop and make a phone call because we're late for a plane. You see the guy in the back seat trying to get his clothes on? He overslept. But then we just decided to keep going." The cop listened to all this. Okay, just drive safely, he told us, and let us go.

So now we were on this highway going as fast as the car would go. I thought we were either going to die or get arrested. We were on this wild freeway ride with all these open coffee containers in the car, and, of course, when the driver had to hit the brakes, the coffee went all over the floor. And, all over us.

Finally, we careened into the airport and roared up to the private hangar. It was now twenty-five minutes past six. At that point it was screw the rental car; we jumped out and ran to the plane. The CEO was just standing there. It turned out we couldn't take off until seven, he said. There was some problem. It was out of our control. So there we were. Coffee all over us, looking awful. And we've damned near killed ourselves getting there. But, of course, the CEO would never know.

ANONYMOUS A

-8-

International Projects:
Different Rules Apply

"Can you meet me in Lima?"

RAY EPICH

Consultants do much of our work for love of the job, but sometimes it's mainly for the sake of the firm. Somehow, international projects seem to account for many of these types of "sacrifices." For instance, finding yourself sucking on oxygen bottles in the middle of the night, high up in the Andes on a mining company project, or spending the days passing frog-selling locals on the roadside who look suspiciously zonked on coca leaves. All the time, reminding each other, "Remember, we're doing this for the firm."

In today's global economy, international consulting has grown more and more prevalent. It can be among the most diverse and rewarding of experiences in the consulting repertoire. It can also be trying or, on occasion, even harrowing. Here, different rules apply. You're dealing with different business cultures, different expectations, and different sets of problems. In some countries, for example, seeking outside consulting services might be looked upon as an admission of failure. Something must be going wrong with that company! Accordingly, a consultant might learn that selling a project by sharing what the firm did for a past client is considered inappropriate, and a sure way not to clinch the sale.

Elsewhere, the business culture might have weaker traditions of using consultants, being less inclined to believe any consultant knows more than they do. How to overcome such mindsets becomes a different kind of challenge. There can be other hurdles to leap, too. Like mandatory evenings spent together carousing and imbibing, as a right of passage to the client's trust, if also the next morning's regret.

Basically, different rules apply and you have to be prepared. From South Korea to Russia, Mexico, Uganda and beyond, here our contributors tell us how they survived crossing geographic and cultural barriers.

Going Where the Money Is

Our firm got into overseas work by accident. A good friend of mine went to Europe to run their Italian operation. While he was there he ran into a problem, so he asked me to come over for a couple of weeks to help out. That was the birth of our international practice, which is now close to 40 percent of our revenue.

It was purely opportunistic. We were sitting around the office looking for work when this call came through; I asked him if he wanted me there tomorrow or the day after. We ended up being there for four weeks and probably did what amounted to the equivalent of a 90-day consulting engagement. We were working six, seven days a week to make an impression.

Frankly, in a small firm I don't know how you can be really strategic in your thinking. Think about it. What's the first thing you need to do? You need to feed your family. So what kind of work will you do? As long you're competent, anything that comes along. Where will you do it? Well, if you don't have anything to do and someone calls from Italy, you'll be happy to go to Italy. If they call from Passaic, New Jersey, you'll go to Passaic.

It's not strategy that drives your firm, its opportunity. You're reacting to the market. What does that mean? Well, somebody called from Italy, so we went to Italy. We were hungry. We found when we were over there that the foreign banks were far behind the U.S. banks. American consultants were also very popular over there. So we found ourselves with more and more opportunities. Typically, about 40 to 50 percent of our revenue now comes from overseas. One year it was as high as 60 percent. They're very nice engagements, too.

In the Middle East and in Turkey we've built a very good name as the consulting firm for corporate banks. In Turkey, we've dealt with just about every major bank. I think we've dealt with most of the banks in the Middle East. In the Arab countries, once you get a reputation they'll pass you around because everything is so interrelated in terms of family connections.

That's what I mean by being opportunistic. You get an opportunity, you go do it. You do a good job and you build on it. We knew the type of business we wanted to do, which was operations analysis. That's what we were good at. That's what we wanted to build on. Outside of that we had no preconceived notions of where we were going to end up.

CARL LOBUE

Resistance to Paying for Advice

Some Asian corporations are not used to paying for advice. It's much easier to sell to Western companies that are already doing business in those countries. However, attitudes are changing and there is more recognition among corporate leaders that there might be some valuable lessons to learn from Western companies. This is especially true in the technology areas or other new industries where they have less experience. But historically there has been a barrier or resistance to paying for advice. It's just not something some cultures are used to doing.

In Korea, there are large, traditional business networks called chaebols. They exist in Japan, too. They represent highly diversified, self-contained operations, some of which have interests virtually throughout the economy. These traditional networks can make it far more difficult for Western consultants to break into certain areas. The thinking is, there's nobody out there who knows more than they do.

If you've been running a shipping business for 40 years, for example, backed up by one of these large networks, you're not likely to think anyone can come close to your level of expertise. But if we're talking about cellular, cable TV, or a new semiconductor area, that is where they are much more willing to look to the West for advice.

WAYNE COOPER

Wear Your National Cufflinks

I headed up our activities in Europe for three years, and it's a practice in Europe to usher visitors into the boardroom because they don't have lobbies like we do here in the States. On one occasion, I was in Switzerland waiting in this company's boardroom. There happened to be a big blackboard in the boardroom, and I couldn't help but notice from what was written there that they were discussing a distribution problem.

Well, when I got in to see the president, I mentioned that one area we were very active in was the area of physical distribution, helping companies decide where to locate warehouses and so on. He said that's exactly the problem we have, I'd like to have you talk with our head of marketing. So just like that I was meeting with the head of marketing. Now this fellow happened to be from Sweden, and that morning I had put on some cufflinks with the three crowns of Sweden on them. I recall telling this fellow that as

I had put on my cufflinks, I said to myself that I thought I might meet some-body from Sweden today. Well, we ended up getting a big assignment on just that chance meeting. By the way, the information on the blackboard wasn't confidential. In fact, it didn't mean anything to me. Other than that I knew they were having a discussion about distribution.

Over the years, I think I can attribute much of my success in business development to my ability to recall assignments we had in a given industry or in a given neighborhood. If a prospect happened to be in an area where we'd done some previous work, sharing that information with them could help sell the project. But in Europe, especially in Germany, it was consid-ered revolting to discuss the name of a client you'd worked for. In Germany, having it known that a company was using a consultant was like having a diphtheria sign on a house. It implied there was something wrong, and you'd better stay away.

ROBERT HAMMAN

DILBERT: © Scott Adams/Dist. By United Feature Syndicate, Inc.

Differences In Perspectives

Early in my years as President of AMCF, I was making the rounds and meet-ing our members in Europe. I was very much struck by the differences in perspective. It was astounding actually how the characters and the personalities of different cultures played themselves out, especially in terms of what I learned about the perceptions of consulting among clients. As Americans, we tend to think of Europe as a monolith. We might differentiate Eastern Europe from Western Europe, but generally we tend to think of Europe mostly in terms of how it differs from us. But actually the culture of things varies considerably across Europe, from country to country.

In the Netherlands, for example, (and these are gross generalities, of course), measurement consulting is very much sought after by corporations. It's very much accepted that you have management consultants help you with your business. People are very open about that. They readily exchange ideas and help each other. But in Germany, by comparison, it's a common characteristic that businesspeople prefer to handle their own problems. Management is embarrassed about having someone help them. Consequently, consulting tends to be more of a quiet-behind-the-scenes enterprise. That leads, of course, to different ways of marketing your services.

In the United States, in comparison to Europe, we tend to be more aggressively innovative, leading edge, and quick to make snap decisions. Europeans look at us and think we don't place enough emphasis on the creation of relationships. We're quicker to call in our quick fix. Have somebody come fix it. So how management consulting is perceived by corporate leaders remains very culturally bound. It's a very interesting thing.

ELIZABETH KOVACS

Join Consulting Firm, Travel to Asia, Throw Up

One hard lesson that I learned in certain Asian countries is that many clients expect you to get drunk with them if you are to gain their trust. The assumption is that everybody can put on a good front, but if you drink with them, they can get past the veneer, and see the real you.

I recall one night in Korea, back in my hotel room after such an evening with a client. The night ended with me sitting on the bathroom floor, leaning into the toilet, thinking that this was way beyond the call of duty. At that point I didn't recall any promises in the recruiting brochure, "Come join a consulting firm, travel, visit exotic places, throw up."

Actually, Korea is among the more unusual places I've ever visited. Korean companies work half a day on Saturdays. That's the norm. Of course, as a consultant I have always worked hard, probably harder than most of my clients whether they were in Italy or Korea. But the expectation of work was far higher in Korea.

At the end of one of our project engagements, we had a huge banquet dinner, with all kinds of exotic foods being served. The sea cucumbers as they were called were quite good. In fact, I ate several of them, assuming they were vegetables. Then I found out the sea cucumbers were actually sea snails. That's when I started to feel a little bit ill.

Then there was the banquet I attended in China where they served chicken in something like a deep sea batter. When I took the batter off one piece with my chopsticks, I found myself staring at the head of a chicken, the entire head! Fortunately, I hadn't yet bitten into it. I knew I wasn't going to eat that particular piece. So I ate the rest of my meal, and then announced how full I was.

In contrast, I spent a year in Milan on a project, and that was certainly among the more pleasant. Our Italian clients had a nice balance to their work and personal lives. They made us leave by 6 o'clock every night, and they liked to take us out to dinner. They had a zest for life, and were very enjoyable to be around.

WAYNE COOPER

A Few Hurdles Along the Way

I remember the first time we worked in Greece; it was a downsizing engagement for a major bank. The Greeks were very pro-union and socialist, and when our guy arrived with his assignment, the union people at the bank were able to have a warrant sworn out for his arrest. The pretext was that he didn't have the proper work permit. Someone tipped him off and he started changing hotels every week, and he moved around the bank a lot to do his work. He became a moving target, dodging the Greek authorities for six weeks until the engagement was completed.

On international projects, you can run into a lot of things that you would never expect. The Saudis have a habit with expats or foreign workers of taking away their passports when they enter the country. That way the Saudis can keep the expats there until they are ready to let them leave. Also, if they want to deport them, they already have their passports.

When I first went there, the Saudi immigration personnel wanted to keep my passport, and I got into a big argument with this bureaucrat at the airport. "You're not taking my passport, I said. He insisted that they always take the passports. But I was adamant. "I'll decide when I leave the country, not you." So they called up the president of the bank, who told them to leave me alone, that I was not just a temporary worker. But I was ready to turn around and leave, right there on the spot. I was not giving my passport to anyone.

If nothing else, the foreign travel is always interesting. Sometimes it's just the little things like watching TV in Saudi Arabia with all the movies censored. You might be watching a movie and some kissing scene would be blacked out. Any kind of word that was off-color would be blacked out. All that has changed now. Everybody has satellite dishes now, so the government can't really censor completely. They do have a law that you're not allowed to have satellite dishes, but if you take a drive down the road you'll see everyone's got a satellite dish.

We have tried to stay out of places where there is government upheaval. Over the years we did a lot of work in India, for example, but there was a period when we wouldn't go there. We wouldn't go to Pakistan, either. In fact, we did a proposal for a big job for Pakistan's federal revenue service, just before a big political blow up there. Then we had to say no. They were killing Americans. We're not going back. In circumstances like that, I'm not sure they could pay us enough.

Nonetheless, we have found ourselves in some thorny situations. When we were doing work for a U.S. bank in Korea, the unions, who are devoted and active, came in and sat down, put on blindfolds, folded their hands and just sat there. All day long they sat there blindfolded. It was a sit-in strike. I never did figure out why they were striking.

One weekend, they actually locked the American business manager in his office on a Friday afternoon. They didn't let him out until Monday morning. When we got through that project we left and never went back. We've been asked back. But we won't go. It's not worth it.

Then again, we've worked in other places like Singapore where they give national awards for productivity. It is great working over there. Everyone wants to win the national award for productivity. They are also completely open about looking for more effective ways to do things. Business gets a lot of support from the government.

Fortunately, we never have had anything of a really serious nature happen on an overseas engagement. That is, other than the couple of stories I've mentioned and perhaps having the opportunity to eat monkey brains or repack your luggage at gun point.

CARL LOBUE

The Ukrainian Privatization Diet

My first overseas client was a privatization committee appointed by the government of the Ukraine. I was 25 at the time. We were hired to help them figure out how to move from mass government ownership into actually creating profitable companies and selling shares to the public. We were building that part of our business, and at that time it was fun work. But, in return, it required a strong commitment and really heavy work to win projects in foreign countries.

The project was about half done by the time I got there. The head of the previous team had been fired; he managed to run up huge bills in his final days, so we had almost no budget money left. But rather than destroy our firm's credibility in the Ukraine, management and staff called together two emergency teams to fix things up. I went out as a junior member of a three-person team.

We had so little money that we had to stay in a modest family-style apartment. It had three bedrooms, so we each had one bedroom and there was a tiny little kitchen in the middle. The three of us were living in fairly close quarters. It was one other man, one woman and me, and the man and woman didn't get along at all. The place had this musty old furniture and I slept on a bed that had spent most of its life as a Styrofoam sofa. There was a long seam running down the middle so you had to sleep on one side or the other.

There was a lift but it was often broken, so we had to walk up and down four flights of stairs. Electricity was reasonably consistent, but not so water. One morning I was taking a shower when the water suddenly went down in the toilet and then right back up, and the water began flooding in. It was in the middle of winter so it was freezing cold at the time and the temperature was about 15 or 20 degrees below zero.

I bought one of those big fur hats the Kremlin guards wear, a big heavy coat, long underwear, and thick gloves. A Western business suit is absolutely useless in that kind of weather. We had a driver of an old Soviet-era car with musty upholstery of unknown origin.

There were no restaurants to speak of in all of the Ukraine as far I could tell, but that was okay, because we didn't have any project money either. Our diet consisted of cheese, kielbasa, a kind of mealy bread and maybe a few jaundiced-looking pieces of fruit. By the time one of my colleagues came out to see me, he said I looked like I'd lost about 15 pounds.

The morale among workers was low in the Ukraine. There was massive over-employment, which is typical of a Soviet-era agency. As many as eight people were crammed into these tiny offices but they really had no work to do, which is really just soul-destroying.

A lot of people ran their own businesses full-time, while working for the government. Here's a good example of this sort of cottage industry. We were promised office space on our client's premises because we were working out of our apartment and we really wanted a place to go and spread out a little bit and not be in each other's faces all the time. We managed to twist someone's arm after about a month and a half, and he came and showed us up into this converted attic. That's where they were going to put us. He opened the door and there was an impromptu hair salon where some people from this government agency were moonlighting.

In the end, the reforms we put forth were blocked by Bolshevik forces in the government. The entire project was absolute hell!

MISHA CORNES

Peru Part 1: Can You Meet Me In Lima?

Nick Radell, a partner, and I were doing a project for a copper and brass company down in St. Louis. A system controller in New York called and asked if we could come to New York to talk about another study.

We said of course, and off we went. His name was Ken Maynard, the same as the famous old Western movie star, so he was easy to remember. Ken said, "I've got a problem in our mine down in Peru. We have an accounting system, we have a planning system, but it's all obsolete. The government is threatening to nationalize the mines and we need a new system to help with valuations and negotiations. How would you fellows propose to work on something like that? Do you do those kinds of studies?"

"Well, of course, we do those kinds of studies," we told him – "we're experts." In fact, we had just put in a new accounting system at his St. Louis plant using one of our staff who was an expert at cost accounting.

We talked to Maynard on a Thursday, and he said, "I'm going down to Lima, Peru on Monday. Could you fellows join me there on Monday?" Now, here is a fellow who's only an assistant controller in a large company. So we're saying to ourselves, we might be going on what could be a wild goose chase, and spend a lot of money flying down to Lima without seeing someone higher than an assistant controller to authorize a project. If we question his authority to do this, of course, we're never going to get this assignment. So we've got to weigh this in our minds. And we didn't have visas. We had passports, but no visas.

We said we had to think about it for a little bit. Nick and I talked in the hallway about what we should do, and I said that this guy has a lot of confidence even though he's a young guy, perhaps 26 years old. He doesn't look like he's going to ask anybody's permission to do this, so why don't we just go down. Then we ask Maynard if he can get us visas. "Oh, yeah," he said, "we have big connections with the Peruvian government. We own these mines down in Lima."

Maynard made the arrangements—I think that we also talked him into paying for the trip as well. He told us to wear old clothes, not to get dressed up. We were looking at one another, wondering how long we are going to be there. The smelter was 250 miles from Lima and the mine was another 100 miles beyond that. The mine was a famous mine, the Cerro de Pasco mine, and it was the first mine that the Incas had in Peru. It was still a working mine hundreds of years later.

RAY EPICH

Peru Part 2: Planes, Chickens and Oxygen Bottles

We flew down, and that was a real experience in those days. You had to fly to Miami from New York. First Chicago to New York, New York to Miami, and in Miami you had to get on an American flight that flew into Lima. And these flights back and forth to South America were just full of people, chickens, just about everything imaginable. And in those days there were no limits on how much you could carry on in terms of baggage, so there were people all around us with sacks, not luggage, but bags of stuff they bought in the U.S. Everything possible!

There were a couple of bathrooms in the back of the plane, and after about seven hours of people going back and forth to these johns, there was water all over the floor. The whole plane was a complete mess. Food wrappers, diapers, an unbelievable mess.

We landed in Lima, and right away we went to our hotel. We were essentially tapped out. The next morning we went over to the client's office in Lima. The staff was a bunch of expatriate accountants—career nomads, expats who worked wherever in the world there is mining. They got very high pay, and six months leave every few years to go back to England.

There was Ken Maynard and he looked like George of the Jungle. He wore a pith helmet and one of these khaki suits with multiple pockets, like someone from South Africa would look on a safari. One of our drivers came up and with a vehicle that looked like a Humvee. It was wider than a normal jeep and longer. Nick and I get in to the back seat, alongside two oxygen bottles. That was our first clue that we were in trouble. The bottles were five, six feet high. Giant oxygen bottles, one on each side. Maynard sat in the front with the driver, and off we went from Lima.

When we planned this trip, we had to line up other players to bring with us. We figured we would bring other players along and somehow slip out so we wouldn't have to do the work ourselves. We definitely did not want to stay up on the mountain forever, obviously. And we had to find people who could handle the altitude. So we found a Swiss in our New York office—he was also a mountain climber—and from Mexico City we brought one of the local staff who was already living at one mile high. We thought those would be the ideal guys to bring along, and they did have the right technical background. They were in another vehicle coming up with us.

For about the first ten minutes we were on level ground. And then the driver put it into low gear, and we started up the mountain. And we were driving, and driving, and driving. We were going up into the Andes on what was never wider than a two-lane road, and sometimes there was only one lane. And as we were driving there were a lot of these blind corners where the driver had to honk the horn, floor it, and try to make it around the corner.

RAY EPICH

[229]

Peru Part 3: Crosses, Coca Leaves, and Llamas

I can't stand to be a passenger in a car in the first place and I didn't dare open my eyes on some of those corners, especially those where there were crosses and little shrines (a blessed virgin with flowers and a cross) which of course memorialized earlier fatal accidents. We didn't see anybody for the first hundred miles but eventually we started to see native Peruvians standing by the road. There were women who looked just like the Peruvian women in National Geographic. They had the big hats, the shawls, just standing there just looking forlorn and chewing betel nuts or coca leaves. I think that they were all zonked out; they just didn't look right. Essentially they were all high, standing along the side of the road. There were no villages, all we saw were these solitary people, all zonked out. Every once in a while we'd also see a llama standing by the side of the road.

This ride went on and up until we reached a pass called Ticlio. As I recall the pass is about 14,000 feet high. Then we realized what the oxygen was for. We started sucking on the oxygen, not continuously but everyone once in a while, just a little whiff.

We passed through Ticlio pass and started down the other side of the mountain to about 13,500 feet. Eventually we got to a town called Arraya where there was a smelter, a big railroad yard, and a building called the Inca Hotel, which was owned by the mining company.

Nick and I both had suitcases. But as we got out of the car, we could hardly even pick them up. We were now suffering from soroche, which is altitude sickness, and we both got headaches real quick.

These Peruvian guys were all about five feet tall – four foot ten or five feet – with barrel chests, clear evidence that Darwin's evolution was at work. Their lungs had expanded over the generations in order to get enough oxygen in the thin mountain air. Apparently, if they went down to Lima they suffered from lung congestion. It is too humid and there is too much oxygen for them, so they have to stay on the mountain top. They worked at the mine or around the Inca Hotel.

RAY EPICH

Peru Part 4: If We're So Smart, What Are We Doing Here?

When we finally checked into the Inca Hotel, they gave us two adjoining rooms with a single bathroom. We went to dinner, and had the hotel's pièce de résistance, roast cuy, a kind of guinea pig. It tasted just like chicken, as you might expect. The one thing they told us was: don't have any alcohol, don't have a beer, just don't drink because this would only accentuate the soroche. So all I had was iced tea. The fellows who were with us were already looking at one another like: "What is this? How did they get us up here?"

We finally went to our rooms at about 8 o'clock in the evening. Again, there were giant oxygen bottles and masks in the room. Nick and I were in one room, there was a shared bathroom in middle, and the other two, Hans the Mexican and Tomas the Swiss, were in the other room. I went to sleep but woke up at 2:00 a.m. with this unbelievable headache. I reached for the oxygen bottle and began sucking on the oxygen. I looked over at the next bed and there was Nick, sitting on the edge of the bed, also sucking oxygen. There was a light on in the bathroom, and the door was not closed. So we went in there, knocked, and found Tomas lying on the floor with a nose bleed and a rag over his face, crying. And Tomas was the guy who already lived at 5,000 feet! The other guy, Hans, was in the bedroom sitting on the edge of the bed, sucking the oxygen.

I went back into the bedroom, sat down, and sucked on my own oxygen. Nick said to me, "If we're so smart, what are doing in a place like this?"

And I told Nick, "This is for the cause, the firm. We're going to get this job." And we had the right crew there, except Tomas of course, he was gone.

We couldn't use anyone who cried the first day. Can you imagine what he'd be doing at the end of a week or two? He'd be outside of our room with a pick axe from one of the workers.

RAY EPICH

Peru Part 5: Down the Shaft

We got up at about 5 o'clock the next morning. Between the smelter and the mine was a one-car train, and inside the coach were four little picnic baskets. They were brown with a checkered table cloth over the top and a bottle of wine sitting up. It looked like we were in Italy having a picnic on the beach on the Riviera.

We headed off to the Cerro de Pasco Mine—I think it was about 150 miles and it took two or three hours on the little train. We were up so high that the lakes didn't have fish in them; there was not enough oxygen at that altitude. But there were frogs, giant frogs. We were seeing more and more natives by the side of the road and there were women standing by the side of the train holding up the frogs by the legs, offering them for sale. We couldn't figure out whether we were to eat them raw or cook them, or maybe take them back to our rooms as pets. But of course we just waved.

The Cerro de Pasco mine is at a 14,000 foot altitude. We went to the mine office, met the foreman, and everybody shook our hands. Then they took us on a mine tour. The full-length coverall suits they gave us were made for guys five feet tall, with big chests. When we finally struggled into these suits, we were hunched over and singing soprano. The elevator took us down the mine shaft to the main floors at 12,000 feet, or nearly 2,000 feet underground. It was unbelievable down there. All I could think about was an earthquake, which does happen all the time. What kind of a chance would you have 2,000 feet underground in the Andes?

In the mine, there was a principal shaft and probably another shaft parallel to that, and large rooms where they stored equipment. The mine was honeycombed with main tunnels and little tunnels shooting of at angles, and air shafts called chimneys that went between the tunnels. Everywhere there were little metal ladders. Only a few of the tunnels had little railroad cars.

They gave us a guide, another five-foot tall guy, whose job was to take us through the tunnels and auxiliary tunnels and up and down the chimneys. He was moving fast, and we were having a hard time keeping up with him. We were crouched down and the tunnels all smelled like urine. The smell was really bad down there because of the urine and the fact that there was very little oxygen inside the mine.

After an hour, we were panting, ready to fall over. Then it dawned on us that our guide wasn't the same guy we started with. They were switching off on us, to keep a fresh leader in front of us, to wear us down. It wouldn't have taken much of a trek to tire us out but they were actually doing some kind of a relay race with always someone fresh in front of us, running up and down these ladders. We had to tell the guide, "Slow down. You're killing us. You're never going to get us out of this mine." They very much enjoyed showing us how hard they work.

We finally got back to the surface and as we unzipped those little suits our voices returned to normal. As we got back on the train to Arraya we still had these tremendous headaches. We were sucking hard on the oxygen bottles. For some reason they didn't have oxygen in the mine. Once we got down to 12,000 feet, I guess they figured we didn't need oxygen anymore.

RAY EPICH

Peru Part 6: Adios, Gimble

The mining people then patted everybody on the back and saluted us for making the valiant effort to tour the mine. And we got the assignment. We identified Hans as a keeper and got rid of Tomas. That night Nick and I were sitting in our room again, wondering, "Now how are we going to get someone to take our place, because we are not coming back here unless it's once a month. But we're not going to be here much if we can help it."

Nick said, "How about Gimble?" He was the one who had done the accounting project in St. Louis. He also had just been married.

And I said, "You know, Gimble's not stupid. Gimble's not coming here."

"Gimble will do anything for money," said Nick.

"Yeah, you're probably right," I said. So we left for the States. Nick calls Gimble and offers Gimble the whole fee, we wouldn't take a cut off the top or anything. The entire fee would go to Gimble. He'd stay down there for 18 months, and once you're out of the country for 18 months you don't have to pay U.S. taxes. So he would get the fee for the whole 18 months, tax-free.

Well, that got Gimble's attention and he agreed. He took his new bride, moved down there, and stayed there for 18 months. We couldn't believe it because around the Inca Hotel were houses where the managers lived. In front of each house there were dressed chickens hanging, or sides of llama, or whatever meat they had, all covered with flies. We thought to ourselves, "This is what people are eating here. They're rubbing the flies off this meat and eating that for 18 months. No thank you." There's no amount of money in the world that would have gotten me to do that. It could have been $10 million, and I still wouldn't have stayed for 18 months on top of that mountain. Nick and I alternated—I think we each went down for a week per month for the first few months. Once Gimble was settled in, we said, "Adios, Gimble."

But Gimble stayed. He not only did that job, he did another job: a linear programming study where we did ore optimization. They had five mines, and they would sell contracts to Europe plus certain assay value for the ore. And if you mixed it properly from the five mines—absolutely met all the criteria but no more than meet the criteria—you'd optimize the ore shipments for millions of dollars of savings. We did a lot of work for them; it was very successful.

RAY EPICH

"It's a whole different world over here, isn't it?"

Out After Dark In Uganda

I was assigned to a Ugandan telecommunications project. The phone company was a state-owned monopoly and we were working on a project to introduce competition. I was staying in the Sheraton in Kampala, the capital. The Sheraton is on a hill away from the rest of the city and I decided that it would be nice to get out of the hotel and take a walk. It was Sunday evening and already dark.

Uganda is right on the equator. And in the tropics, they get more or less 12 hours of daylight and 12 hours of darkness every day. So no matter the time of year, it gets dark around 6:00 p.m. As I walked along, this prostitute was staring at me and waving. She was wearing bike shorts and a skin-tight top; she was positively overflowing from both. She was just a big woman, she certainly outweighed me. (Editor's Note: Misha would acknowledge that he is in fact skinny.)

Anyway, I passed her by. By that time it was getting too dark to walk back, so I turned around to look for a taxi. But this woman took it as a sign that I was just too shy to approach her and came up and grabbed the front of my pants really hard. She said something like, come on handsome. I was just shocked and very embarrassed.

I just ran away. I was frightened. Plus, you never know, she probably wasn't working alone. It was probably the best thing to do in the situation.

MISHA CORNES

On the Road in St. Petersburg

The first time I went to Russia was actually before the collapse of the Soviet Union. I was working in Helsinki and, just for the experience, decided to take the 45 minute flight over to Leningrad (now St. Petersburg). I arranged a four- or five-day trip through In-Tourist, what was then the Soviet Tourist Bureau. As luck would have it, that happened to be the same week that the Korean airliner, KAL 007, was shot down by a Soviet jet.

My wife was back in North Carolina, and, needless to say, she did not want me to go. But I'd already invested a few bucks with In-Tourist and it seemed to me to be a very interesting opportunity. I did call the U.S. Embassy in Helsinki just to check on the situation. I remember being routed to five different bureaus within the embassy before anyone would talk to me directly. Finally, I got through to someone at the political section and asked them if there had been any incidents involving U.S. citizens. The answer was no. But they cautioned me that there was an embargo on, and no U.S. air carriers were going into Russia. They recommended that I not go.

Of course, Finn Air was still flying into Russia, which was what I was booked on. I told the embassy I was still considering going. They repeated their recommendation that they would rather that I didn't. I remember asking them, are you telling me that I can't go? Well, no, as a U.S. citizen, I could do exactly as I liked. They just strongly recommended that I not make the trip. Needless to say, I ignored their advice and off I went to Russia. It seemed to me to be an interesting time to be there.

So there I was, a party of one and one of the very few Americans in St. Petersburg at the time. I saw the English translation newspaper posted in the hotel with the Russian position on the airliner incident, which I immediately discounted as complete propaganda. I was also harassed by the wife of a Moscow embassy staff member who was herself traveling as a tourist in Russia. She thought it was inappropriate that I was there, but as it turned out she had her college roommate with her, who was obviously doing the same thing I was.

St. Petersburg is considered the most beautiful city in Russia, the Venice of Russia. But actually I found it to be incredibly dirty. At the hotel I was staying at the water basically ran yellow. The TV didn't work and each hall was guarded by an old dragon woman in a black dress, who just sat there staring sternly at everyone who walked down the hall. The old women in the chairs were the result of a socioeconomic policy to create work. You would find the streets being swept by the same women, with their black dresses and twig brooms.

The most exciting moment was when I became lost. I had left anything having to do with business back in Helsinki, in a locker at the airport. That meant I also left behind my maps of the city. There were no English translation signs anywhere. I knew the Teniski Prospect, which is a main street in St. Petersburg but otherwise I had to rely on my memory of the maps. Generally, I got around okay but on one occasion I did become hopelessly lost.

When I realized I had no idea where I was, I figured the young people would probably have better command of the English language than the older people, so I stopped two teenage girls on the street to ask directions. They didn't have any English language skills. But the armed soldier nearby did. He came up to me to ask what I was doing. I think he suspected I was trying to pick up these girls but I was really just trying to find my street. He was your stereotypical stern Russian solider, never cracked a smile even when I put on my best Southern charm. He had his rifle at the ready, off his shoulder, but he did tell me how to get to where I was going.

I also met a fellow on the street who wanted to practice his English. He came up to me and I thought he wanted money or to buy my blue jeans or something like that. Many Russians on the street wanted to buy some American item. Oddly enough, all I had with me was The Nine Hundred Days of Leningrad, by Harrison Salisbury, which is about the siege of Leningrad during World War II. This was probably not the wisest book to have taken into Russia. Well, I ended up being invited to some nightclub with this fellow and his friends and out of curiosity I went. I thought it would be interesting just to hang around with a bunch of Russian people, to spend some time with them.

It turned out some of the women there were prostitutes plying their trade. Of course, I wasn't interested in anything except buying some drinks and talking. There was quite a bit of discussion about Bolshevism that night. Two of these guys were royalists and they were not at all happy with Communism. They were also vehemently anti-Semitic. It was just a very strange political conversation and it went on almost all night.

Eventually the night became quite late and in St. Petersburg they raise the bridges at about three in the morning and they stay up until about five in the morning. There is a lot of water, so in that sense it's almost like Venice. I knew I had to get back to my hotel before they raised the bridges. I ended up weaving my way back to the hotel with these two royalists, one of whom spoke English very well and one of whom did not speak English at all. On the way back to the hotel the fellow who didn't speak English started screaming something in Russian. I asked the other fellow what he was saying. He said, "Oh, he's just saying that all Bolsheviks should be hung from the nearest lamppost." This had me more than a little worried because in Leningrad the police were likely to take offense. At this point I said, "Well, fellas, it's been a lot of fun but good night." By then I could see the area where my hotel was. I made a hasty departure and that was my last contact with those guys.

As a postscript, I had planned to meet the English-speaking fellow the next evening, but it never happened. We were going to meet at this big plaza. I went at 6:30 pm, the appointed time, and it was misting slightly so I wore my trench coat. There were about 15 other people skulking around this plaza, also in their trench coats. Across the plaza was this government building where I could see video cameras pointing out the windows toward the area. I waited around for about 20 minutes before deciding maybe this wasn't such a good idea. So I just went back to my hotel, had a nice quiet dinner and left the next day.

On the way out of the country, the guard at the airport took considerable interest in my book, The Nine Hundred Days. He was fascinated with it and kept turning the pages, but he wasn't reading it. I guess he was looking for microdots or something. Then very sternly he gave it back to me. I returned to Finland on Aeroflot, the Russian airline which was not considered to be particularly safe. I remember the entire planeload of passengers burst out in spontaneous applause when the plane lifted off. The relief was palpable. And that ended my first trip to Russia.

JERRY JACKSON

Flying Over the Jungles of Java

I had an engagement in Indonesia that was unique and a lot of fun. It involved an Indonesian company buying a major U.S. company. Because the Indonesian government was involved in helping guarantee some loans, I had to meet with a senior government executive who would be the equivalent of our Secretary of Commerce. While I was there, this client wanted to show us his other operations, so in Jakarta I found myself climbing aboard a helicopter. We flew around Java and it was a hoot.

We flew into these small villages where the kids would all be let out of school and they'd rush up to the helicopter. They'd kind of bow to the guy from the company because all their fathers worked for the company. I've probably done other projects that were more professionally exciting. But flying over the jungles of Java! God, that was beautiful. Something I won't forget soon.

MICHAEL LAPORTA

Kuwait Part 1: What Are You Doing Next Week?

I was sitting in our Chicago office one Friday afternoon, wrapping up the week's business when the phone rang. My boss was in New York and wanted me to come there Monday morning and meet some potential clients. "Sure, I said, who are they?' He told me they were the Al Ghanim family from Kuwait and the project involved building a strategy for investing their money throughout the world.

The members of the family and their large coterie all were gathered in a huge living room in the Presidential Suite at the Plaza Hotel. I was ushered to the front and the questions began. They were different from me in looks, attitudes, demeanors, etc. I was lost as to how to fit into this group as well as to how to execute the project. But somehow I was accepted and invited to Kuwait. Because westerners had difficulties in adjusting and in being useful there the invitation was simply to come out at their expense and spend a week with them. At the end of the week I could tell them whether I wanted to stay.

At that time the only country outside the U.S.A. that I had been to was Canada and this was back in the days when our border was completely open. In fact, I didn't even have a passport. But, all the details were arranged and off I went. My first stop was our London office where the partner-in-charge was responsible for our work in Kuwait. He briefed me and we blocked out a study plan including a schedule for rotating back and forth between Chicago, London and Kuwait.

I landed in Kuwait and while waiting for my bag at the airport, my trench coat was stolen. I swear that I only blinked and it was gone. A taxi took me to the local hotel where they had booked my reservation. I was the only westerner in the hotel; nobody else spoke English and I didn't know a word of Arabic. Directly outside my window was the loudspeaker for the mosque and six times a day the muezzin would call the faithful to prayers. I jumped to the ceiling each time. After two days, I convinced the client coordinator that moving to the new Sheraton was a condition for my continuing on the project. It was brand new and completely western, and it had liquor service to boot.

RICHARD METZLER

Kuwait Part 2: The Boom Town

Kuwait in 1974 was a boom town, simply exploding with growth and opportunities. In a matter of only a few years, the city was completely transformed. The government tore down the old mud walls that surrounded their city, and transformed it from medieval to modern with gleaming towers, resembling many big cities in Europe or the U.S.A.

The Al Ghanim family was one of the highest ranked families in Kuwait, perhaps second only to the Al Sabah family whose head was the Emir of Kuwait. The Al Ghanims had the largest General Motors dealership in the world in terms of sales. They were in construction, finance and just about every facet of Kuwaiti social and business life. And like most Kuwaitis they were very uncomfortable about the small size of Kuwait and how precarious it was in the Middle East. The country is very small; it had been carved out of Iraq by the British during the 1800's. Kuwaitis were concerned about being invaded and they wanted their money to be safe.

But they also wanted to show to all Kuwaitis that they were a key part of a growing nation and their projects had to be highly visible. Our overall strategy consisted of investing in infrastructure businesses in safe countries in the West, and setting up branches and projects inside Kuwait. One of the first acquisitions was a prefab building company in Texas. Investment in the U.S. had minimum country risk and they could bring the products and technology back into Kuwait for growth.

RICHARD METZLER

Kuwait Part 3: You Can't Take Detroit Out of the Boy

The Kuwaitis had stereotypes of everybody else in the world. They hired only Scots for accounting positions because they were thought to be tight with money. They hired only Americans for strategy and management, and so on. This was important because almost all the workers were expatriates. The Palestinians at that time were the most educated of Arabs and held the key positions as assistants to all the top Kuwaitis. They were the guards and the gatekeepers so to speak. The Al Ghanim family even collected dues from Palestinian workers for the PLO.

I became friends with the Scot who headed the accounting area. His family adopted me and we went to the Arabian Gulf at the Saudi border for swimming and socializing on weekends. He knew a lot about me from our long conversations, such as where I grew up and where I went to school.

One night the young head of the Al Ghanim family invited a large group to his private home on the shores of the Gulf for a dinner with his father and the Managing Director of the old BOAC airline out of London. His home had the only green lawn in the country. He installed a desalinization plant for fresh water and brought in a horticulturist to create the lawn and gardens. His reception room looked huge to me, and the floor was layered with thick Persian carpets. Drinks were being served from a solid gold cart. The dinner tables were thick crystal glass cast in Italy. I was overwhelmed.

During dinner, the Al Ghanim family patriarch told us about his youth and the time he spent on the desert. He was friends with a young Saudi prince who later became the king. They went falconing in the desert and would stay out for weeks in tents. He showed us the scars from when a falcon decided to take a bite from his arm. Literally, he said, in his lifetime Kuwait had moved from a medieval society to a modern nation.

As I was sitting there with my jaw dropped to the floor, my Scottish friend came over and said, "You can take the boy out of Detroit, but you can't take Detroit out of the boy." Truer words were never spoken.

RICHARD METZLER

Me and My Shadow

In some countries, such as Iran just prior to the overthrow of the Shah, it was customary for the government to assign a counterpart who shadowed you around. We had a project director assisting the government in implementing a new telecommunications system, and he and his shadow were in a high-rise office building built for the new telecommunications company. They had gone up to this one floor and got off and were looking for office space for the consulting team. My partner happened to notice that one whole wing of the floor was completely empty. So he asked his Iranian colleague if they could use that space. This fellow says no, that space is reserved for the company cafeteria.

My partner asked him how soon would they be building the cafeteria. Would there be any chance they could use it temporarily, at least until construction of the cafeteria got underway? And the shadow tells him that actually they had no plans to build a cafeteria, they had merely told the employees they were building a cafeteria. But if they used the space even temporarily as an office, then the employees would become suspicious that they had no intention of ever building a cafeteria. Believe it or not, that's how things were done.

I think sometimes it can be pretty tough duty to work in such different cultures. A number of years ago, one of our partners got into a very difficult situation because of a contract dispute. It involved some procedure that had to be followed regarding how a document was signed; something to do with having a third party attest to it. Apparently, this fellow didn't understand how things had to be done and ended up violating this protocol. It turned out to be a serious matter and the next thing he knew he was in jail for over a week. Eventually we got him out with the intervention of the State Department. But after that it was a little hard to find people who wanted to go on that assignment.

We've learned a lot since then. For one thing, we always make sure people work with business agents who understand the local culture. If we don't have a local operation, then we'll find somebody there to partner with who understands the local business practices.

Overseas you have to evaluate carefully exactly what kind of situation you're getting into. There was one account we were working with in Latin America and one of my partners got into a dispute with the client over the settlement of the final fees. The other side suggested we could settle the whole thing by making a certain "financial contribution." The partner said absolutely not, we don't do business that way, never did and never will. We'll litigate instead.

We hired a local attorney, but when our side showed up in court, we discovered it was a military court. The judge was sitting there in uniform, wearing a bandolier and a Sam Brown belt with a gun and holster. Slowly the light went on, and we folded our tent and left the country. We never did collect our fees. It was what you call a learning experience.

Fortunately, the world has changed a lot since those days. Most countries now are more or less up to certain standards in their business practices. But I'm sure there's still someplace in the world where you run into this kind of situation.

DAVID TIERNO

*"Grab some lederhosen, Sutfin. We're about to climb
aboard the globalization bandwagon."*

The Cost of Doing Business

Frankly, I think bribes are the cost of doing business in the developing world. Many firms build that factor into their calculations for project costs. German companies can write off bribes in their accounting books. On the other hand, the U.S. government demands that U.S. firms not pay bribes. But there are lots of other ways to compensate people in order to get business. None of which I would advocate or push for, but these often end up happening.

Probably the most common method is to hire an employee or a temporary employee, usually some local guy who's connected to your client. It could also be their nephew or niece. This isn't necessarily bad because you need someone who understands the local environment. I also assume that I'll be paying exorbitant amounts of money to local consultants, usually though a local company. Typically the one who recommends the local consultant is the client itself.

For instance, we had a project in Tanzania that entailed developing a regulatory agency across six sectors of Tanzanian infrastructure, all of which were owned by the state. We were asked to take on a local man who had served as the first telecommunications regulatory commission chairman in Tanzania. He was basically the equivalent of the head of the FCC and would have been perfect if we could have gotten him. We wanted to hire him to advise us on the regulatory environment in Tanzania, but in fact, he was so good and so successful that he turned up his nose at working with us. This is very rare because the locals don't ordinarily have a chance to get paid by a Western company at Western rates.

Having failed to secure our first choice, our client said, "Oh, we have just the guy for you." And they introduced us to a man with a doctorate, apparently he was an economist. It turned out that he knew nothing about regulation, he was lazy, and he billed outrageous amounts of money for doing basically nothing. I wanted to hire him directly but was forced to hire him as part of a two-person consulting company, which also contributed nothing. We all agreed up front that I had a fixed pool of money that I wanted to pay a consultant, probably around $10,000. I wanted to reserve some of our money for this other superman if and when he became available.

For their purposes they wanted it to look like I was paying them like $500 a day rather than paying them in a lump sum, so that they could use this figure to charge future consultant companies. So imagine my surprise when five weeks into what turned out to be a seven-month project, they billed me for four men, basically for doing some photocopying and production and other odd jobs like that.

It's a form of bribe in the sense that I didn't want to pay these people for the work that not done, or if performed only very badly. But I'm getting direct pressure from the client saying, what have you done about these local guys, they're complaining to me that they haven't been paid. What's the problem? Though the link is not absolutely explicit I understand that there's often some arrangement between the client and the local consultant. In developing countries, people have understandings and look after one another.

MISHA CORNES

Eye-Opening Experiences

One of the most important, life changing events I've ever had was the first time I went behind the Iron Curtain. This was in 1972 on a trip to Hungary and Austria. I was married then to someone with a Hungarian name. His parents were Hungarians. Being behind the Iron Curtain gave me a different appreciation of the world—the trip was actually very scary for me. I had grown up in the 60's when we were in Vietnam and people were burning draft cards. There was a lot of anti-American sentiment around the world. But to go to Hungary in 1972, and have this patriotic feeling coming back to the United States, to be able to appreciate the First Amendment and the Bill of Rights, the Constitution that we live under; well, that stuck with me, very deeply.

I was also in Czechoslovakia two months before the Berlin Wall came down. Again, the sense of dread was there, going over the border, the dogs sniffing the train. You could see trusses above the train where we were sitting. We had been told there were snipers on the trusses who would shoot at random into the coal carts because people would sometimes try to escape by hiding under the coal. There was a sense of desperation in the air then, a feeling that something eventually was going to happen. But it sure didn't seem like we were just two months away from such major change. Traveling does change your view of the world.

ELIZABETH KOVACS